OSCAR THE BIONIC CAT

OSCAR THE BIONIC CAT

A Heart-Warming Tale of
Feline Bravery

Kate Allan

WINDSOR
PARAGON

First published 2013
by Summersdale Publishers Ltd
This Large Print edition published 2013
by AudioGO Ltd
by arrangement with
Summersdale Publishers Ltd

Hardcover   ISBN: 978 1 4713 6325 2
Softcover   ISBN: 978 1 4713 6326 9

British Library Cataloguing in Publication Data available

Printed and bound in Great Britain by TJ International Limited

CONTENTS

CHAPTER 1

A Huge Dilemma

Mike and I are sitting side by side on the sofa. Not talking, not watching television, not listening to music. We are, however, thinking the same thing. What is going to become of our beloved cat? It is touch-and-go whether he is going to make it. It's unbearable to think that our little friend, so placid and loveable, is perilously close to having used up all of his nine lives after such a short time in our company. His destiny is in the hands of the vet who has our complete faith and trust, but whose job is so immense. We can do nothing but wait. No one knows what the outcome will be. This type of surgery has never been done before on this scale. Unanswered and almost unanswerable questions hang in the air. What will happen next? Will he recover properly? Should we even be putting him through this? Since he entered our lives two-and-a-half years ago, Oscar has made us laugh, kept us company, entertained us and comforted us. He has caused us anxiety, panic, concern, fear, distress, financial burden and worry. He has made us question our morals and search deep into our souls. We could never have foreseen what an incredible journey Oscar would go on, with us at his side. He is the most remarkable cat we have ever known.

We sit quietly waiting for news, which may not come today, or tomorrow, or even next week. It seems such a long way from when Oscar first came into our lives.

I must admit I was a little surprised when Mike Nolan, my partner, said he was thinking of getting two little black kittens, a girl and a boy. Although we did not live together, it seemed (to me at least) that we would at some point in the not-too-distant future. We had been dating for about a year and our relationship was going from strength to strength. I had two cats of my own, Buzz and Lou, and I wasn't convinced that when the time came to share, they would be able to tolerate any more cats in the household. They could not stand each other as it was.

I did not force the issue with Mike. He rented a house with Tracey, an old friend, and had two teenage children, Rachael and Christopher, who stayed with him every weekend. For him it was not just a case of upping sticks and moving into my flat. Similarly, I did not want to give up the home that I had worked so hard for and move in with Mike. The ideal solution would be for us to buy a place together, but it was still a little early in our relationship to make that commitment. I worried that if he got the kittens there would be a delay in making our relationship more permanent; but despite my inner reservations, I went along with him.

We sat at the table discussing names. T. S. Eliot wrote in *Old Possum's Book of Practical Cats* that cats must have three names: one for everyday use, one unique name that is theirs alone and one that only the cat itself knows. We were content just to decide on the everyday name. Not that there was a huge debate; Mike was already pretty set on what he favoured.

2

'I really like Oscar for a boy,' said Mike.

'Yes, it's quite majestic and masculine,' I replied.

'No, it's not that . . . I'd quite like to name a cat after that one in America. You know, the one who could sense when people were about to die. Oscar the Death Cat!' he added.

'Nice,' I said sarcastically. I did not know the story of this other Oscar, but when I found out more about it, it really was extraordinary. The cat has lived his whole life at the Steere House Nursing and Rehabilitation Center in Providence, Rhode Island, and has become famous for predicting death. Each day, he patrols the corridors of the Advanced Dementia wing. He enters the patients' rooms and sniffs the air. If he settles on a bed, the doctors alert the patient's family as it means death is imminent. Oscar has curled up with over fifty patients in their dying hours. Rather than finding this unpleasantly morbid, many families have taken comfort from Oscar guiding their loved ones to heaven, and it has enabled them to gather at the bedside to be there for the final moments. One scientific explanation suggests that Oscar detects ketones, biochemicals given off by dying cells on the patient's breath. Others argue that it may just be that in the last hours of life, the patient typically becomes very still and the cat likes the lack of movement. Either way, Oscar stays with them until their final breath is drawn and he is routinely mentioned in obituaries and funeral services.

As for a girl's name, Mike decided on Poppy. It was a light-hearted, sweet name and went well with Oscar. I mused that had Mike and I been lucky enough to have children together, these may have been the names we would have chosen for them.

Personally, as far as cats are concerned, I like non-human names like Cheese and Onion. Tracey used to have a cat called Seefa, which I thought was excellent. I was very much against trend though, with more and more people choosing 'human' names for their pets. A survey by PetPlan in 2009 showed that the top ten names for pets (from those that had taken out insurance policies with them), featured exclusively human names and crossed over significantly with popular baby names. Charlie, Ruby and Jack, for example, featured on both top ten lists. So at eight weeks old, Oscar and Poppy (both top ten names) were ready to be collected and taken to their new home.

They were both black, although Poppy had about six little white hairs on her throat. Oscar, who was fluffier, was entirely black.

Mike put the cat carrier down on the kitchen floor and opened its door. The frightened kittens clung together inside, unsure what to do in these unfamiliar surroundings.

'Come on, little ones,' said Tracey, as she crouched down to encourage them out. I stood behind her waiting for them to emerge.

Poppy was the first to step out and immediately ran to the corner of the room to try to hide. Oscar was hot on her tail and again they huddled up together, literally shaking with fear.

Mike picked them up and tried to make them comfortable on their furry cushion (brought with them from their old house). Whilst they may have been able to smell their mother, she was missing and they clearly wanted nothing more than to have her there. They meowed incessantly, bewildered by their new environment. The three of us stroked them, picked them up, cuddled them and soothed them, but they seemed so distressed it was heartbreaking to watch. They cried out for their mother almost non-stop.

Mike cooked them a small portion of fish and put it in the cat bowls, which seemed disproportionately large for such small kittens. At last they stopped crying and gobbled it down like they had never been fed before, taking huge gulps of the lactose-free cat milk we had also bought. With tummies full, the kittens snuggled together on the cushion, Poppy sucking at her brother's fur until they fell asleep for the first time in their new home.

It did not take long for them to settle in; there was so much to explore. There were two flights of stairs, which led into exciting playrooms full of things to jump on and climb through. At night, for example, they could scale the side of the duvet, preferably pulling it towards the floor at the same time and jump onto the warm person lying underneath it, or partially underneath it by then. Even better fun was to practise hunting skills by watching a person's foot twitch as it poked through the covers . . . then pounce! This inevitably resulted in waking the foot-owner with a start, and causing eight furry little feet to scamper off down the stairs on hearing the scream from the no-longer-slumbering human.

The staircase was another place to have huge amounts of fun. Depending how brave they were feeling, they could jump through the banister from about three feet onto the floor below without hurting themselves.

'Watch me!' Poppy seemed to squeak. 'I'm going

to jummmmp!' and she was through, launching herself fearlessly.

'I'm scared!' Oscar replied, but reluctantly followed her.

'Come with me. Let's try this,' enthused Poppy as she tried to escape, frantically scratching at the glass in the conservatory, without success.

'Will somebody open this door immediately! I need to go out! NOW!' she seemed to say through her meows. Did Oscar assist her? Did he scratch alongside her to aid her quest for freedom? No. Oscar simply watched in awe as his nimble, tenacious sister became increasingly frustrated by the confines of the fortress in which she lived.

Over the next few weeks they grew fast. They were still similar in size and could only be told apart by Oscar's slightly longer fur. Every night they tucked into freshly cooked fish and cat milk, which they consumed with gusto.

'Do you think that maybe they should have fish just now and again as a treat, rather than every night?' I asked when I was round at Mike's one night.

'But they love it,' he replied as he carefully prepared it for them; cooking it, cutting it up and serving it at just the right temperature—neither too hot nor too cold. He was proving to be a very devoted cat-dad. He was right too; they adored it.

Poppy decided, however, that she wanted more variety in her diet. One day, Mike and I, Tracey, Rachael and Christopher were all settling down to Sunday lunch at the table in the conservatory. The roast lamb, roast potatoes, broccoli, carrots and cauliflower were dished out and we each took our preference of mint sauce, mint jelly and/or gravy

6

and began tucking into the weekly feast. Rachael was in the middle of applying for her university place and our conversation revolved around her choices.

'I think I want to do a law-related subject but not pure law,' she said. 'I'd quite like to join the police so I want to do something that might be useful for that.'

Although I'd only known her for a short period of time, I really got a sense of her determination to do the very best she could for herself. Unlike many seventeen-year-olds she seemed to favour staying in and revising than going out partying.

'Have you decided where in the UK you want to study?' I asked. Moving to the UK after living a relatively sheltered life in Jersey can be a culture shock for many young people going to university.

'I think I'll go wherever the best courses are,' she replied in her usual, pragmatic way. Suddenly our conversation was shattered by an enormous crash from the kitchen.

'What was that?' shrieked Chris and we all leapt up from the table to see for ourselves.

We could see straightaway what had happened and fell about laughing. There on the floor was a large broken plate, a half-eaten leg of lamb and Poppy merrily tucking in to her first taste of freshly cooked meat. Unusually, Oscar was nowhere to be seen. Perhaps he had run off, scared by all the commotion.

Mike approached Poppy, but the chances of separating her and her quarry were about as likely as her turning round and asking for potatoes and gravy to go with it. She wolfed it down with relish (not the hamburger sort). Of course, we didn't mind at all. In fact we loved their antics and every time they got into the slightest bit of mischief we were reminded of the joy that kittens bring.

Although Poppy was far and away the bolder of the two, Oscar had his moments. One morning Mike was rustling me up coffee and croissants as a Sunday morning breakfast treat. He laid the table in the conservatory with an assortment of jams, butter, a cafetière of fresh coffee and a jug of chilled orange juice. He even managed to find linen napkins. I was most impressed. The wonderful aroma wafting around the house told us that everything was ready. Mike took the croissants from the oven where they had been gently warming and placed them on the worktop whilst he looked for a basket to put them in. Quick as flash, Oscar, who had appeared from the hall, leapt onto the side, took a croissant in his mouth and jumped back onto the floor. He held the croissant steady with his paw and started gnawing away.

'Poppy!' exclaimed Mike instinctively. Realising his mistake he said, 'Oh it's YOU!' as Oscar continued to boldly nibble away at the croissant. I couldn't help but think that Mike was rather proud of Oscar. I was sure that if he was unhappy with Oscar's behaviour he would have made more of a fuss about having to share the solitary remaining croissant with me. However, he did not complain at all and we both laughed all through breakfast at the latest escapade.

In the autumn, once they had recovered from their respective sterilisation procedures and had their immunisations, a whole new world awaited them. The great outdoors would take their lives in different directions and for Oscar, have

8

far-reaching consequences.

Like all kittens, when Oscar and Poppy made their first foray outside, it was with a mixture of curiosity and trepidation. As usual, Poppy led the way out of the conservatory doors that they had been peering through for months. They jumped down onto the cool slabs of the patio and gingerly padded around, not wanting to run too far from the door. Neither of them seemed quite sure what to do. Now the great freedom they had been hankering after had arrived, it was all a bit scary.

Poppy edged towards the flower bed and sniffed around the base of the rose bush. Oscar followed closely behind, sniffing the air as he familiarised himself with the new smells. Instinctively, Poppy chewed on a blade of grass. Gradually they went deeper into the garden, although they were never more than about six feet from the conservatory door that led back to safety. A seagull flew overhead, squawking as he went, and the kittens looked up with awe. A few moments later, one of the last of the summer's butterflies flew onto the buddleia.

'That looks more like it,' Poppy seemed to be thinking as she scampered over and leapt to catch it. Although she missed, she kept a careful watch to see if the red admiral would return so she could try and make her first kill. It was not her lucky day and after half an hour of wandering around the garden taking in the scents, we brought the two kittens inside.

Once they had been allowed out, that was it; as soon as anyone went in the conservatory they would run to the door and meow to be let out. Their confidence increased with each adventure and before long they were big enough to be allowed out unsupervised. Before they could become fully free-range, they had to learn how to use the cat flap. Tracey stood on one side of the door and Mike on the other side, as they pushed the flap to demonstrate how to open it. The kittens were more interested in watching the movement rather than learning the mechanics of it. Anything that moved was fair game to be pounced on, so instead of using their paws to gain access to the garden, they preferred to grab the human hands. This game went on for several minutes until the futility of it struck Tracey.

'Let's take the flap off and let them practice jumping through the hole,' she suggested. This worked a treat, and as soon as the kittens realised it was an exit point, they were both through. A few days later, when the flap was replaced, such was their eagerness to go and explore, that they pushed it without hesitation, determined to get outside.

Despite having this freedom, Oscar and Poppy still followed each other everywhere, or at least Oscar followed Poppy. They met new cats in the neighbourhood; some were friendly, like Ollie, a big white and tan tomcat from next door. Ollie had also enjoyed the flap-free days and had invited himself in for breakfast. He popped back for dinner and enjoyed curling up on the dining-room chair. The kittens were bemused by his presence, but not hostile. They had too much to do outside to be overly concerned by the older visitor. Anyway, Oscar and Poppy also made themselves at home next door, popping in through Ollie's cat flap to eat his dinner as he'd eaten theirs. A change was as good as a rest after all!

Oscar seemed to enjoy meeting the neighbouring cats but was yet to learn his limitations. One day, a big tabby cat scaled the garden wall and nonchalantly walked along it. 'Wow,' thought Oscar, 'I want to do that!' and he repeatedly tried to jump on top of the wall. As it was about six feet high, and Oscar was so small, it really was a feat beyond him. He was undeterred though and kept jumping, only to land back in the flower bed as his claws failed to grip the wall. The tabby cat strolled on, ignored the pesky kitten and jumped down into the neighbour's garden. Eventually Oscar was distracted by a sparrow and turned his attention to it before the little bird flew off to safety.

Most cat owners will agree that one of the downsides of owning cats is that they instinctively hunt small birds and animals, more for entertainment than for nourishment. It is almost inevitable that as an owner of outdoor cats you will, at some point, be confronted with a dead mouse or fledgling bird. I knew the inevitable day would bring a mix of pride and disgust.

Whilst we like to think that this prey is a 'gift' to make us proud of them, the reality lies more in their inherent instinct to take their kill back to the lair to 'feed the family'. After all, cats are hardly renowned for wanting to please humans. They spend their whole lives demanding that we please them.

The thing about sharing your life with cats is that you can never have too many expectations about what you will get in return. Dogs will bound up to you and show their love, even if you've only returned from popping out to the corner shop to buy a pint of milk. They will whoop with delight when you return from work, wagging their tails and panting breathlessly, as if it is truly the happiest moment of their lives. Cats, on the other hand, may be there when you get in from work, or they may not. They might jump down from the bed to greet you, but they probably won't—unless they're hungry of course. If you head straight to the kettle on your return (or to the wine bottle in the fridge), chances are they might be sniffing around. Not, of course, to comfort you after your presentation went a bit wrong because you'd cleverly designed your PowerPoint slides to include the logo of your potential client only to find, whilst sitting in reception, that they'd rebranded it from orange and purple to navy blue. Dogs will sit there whilst you vent the horrors of the day, looking at you with a love you rarely meet in the human world. Cats, are more like, 'Yeah, well, whatever. Is there any chance of tuna tonight?'

Despite Poppy's dominance in the duo, it was Oscar who was the first to bring back quarry. Mike was witness to this inaugural hunt. Oscar spotted movement by the fence, gnashed his teeth and crouched down, totally still. His prey was also still. Oscar edged forward slowly and quietly, keeping low to the ground. He saw his prey move, pounced, but was too slow and it eluded him.

Mike smiled to himself, like a proud father watching his son walking up the path to his first day of school. He could not see exactly what Oscar had his sights set on, but it was very entertaining to watch his furry black kitten developing from being a playful little bundle into a competent killing machine.

Not to be outdone, Oscar lay in wait, knowing

the kill would be his if he exercised patience and determination. The air was still and all was quiet. A sudden breeze blew through the garden, ruffling Oscar's fur and causing the plants to stir. This was his moment; Oscar pounced and trapped the creature under his paws. Unsure of what to do next, he waited, holding it down, looking around him to make sure no one was going to take it from him. By now Poppy had started to venture out without him and was nowhere to be seen, so he couldn't look to her for help or advice. Not that she would have helped him. When it came to catching prey, it was each man, or cat, for himself. Somehow, Oscar figured he had to move his victim from under his paws to his mouth without setting it free. In one swift movement he separated his paws and swooped down. Success! He had it in his mouth and without hesitation, ran the few feet up the path to the cat flap. This one was coming home! Mike greeted him on the other side of the door, hoping that whatever it was, Oscar wouldn't drop it and send it scurrying through the hall.

'Well done, Oscar,' praised Mike. He had read somewhere that you should never tell cats off for bringing wildlife home as they were only behaving in the way they knew.

Oscar had his prey firmly in his jaws, a long, thin tail hanging out of one side of his mouth.

'Oh dear, Oscar,' said Mike, and started laughing. 'You haven't got a mouse, boy, that's a leaf!'

Oscar dropped his 'kill' and sure enough it was a beech leaf that he had been stalking and ultimately going for with the focus and drive of a trained assassin. As the kitten looked at the leaf, Mike was unsure if Oscar was proud or embarrassed by what he had done. He tossed his tail in the air and walked away as if to say, 'All right Dad, don't take the mickey out of me. I didn't know you were watching.' Mike picked up the dead leaf and threw it back outside. Possibly because of this rather inauspicious start, Oscar never became the greatest mouser in the family.

Christmas brought new joy for the kittens. There was a bounty of new foods to try—ham, turkey, prawns and smoked salmon—and we were not surprised they liked these delicacies. However, when Poppy started to eat the leftover crumbs and mincemeat from a plate of mince pies we thought that maybe we should go to greater lengths to tidy up. The days of leaving festive fayre on the side for us to eat at leisure were over. The trifle could not be let out of sight for a moment. Aside from the food there was also the wonder of the Christmas tree. A real tree in the house! Wow! This was exciting!

This marvellous structure must have been to the kittens, what Disneyland is like for the first time for children. The baubles spun and glinted with the reflection of the fairy lights. The twirled tinsel shimmered around the branches and there was even a little ornamental feathered bird nestled in the tree. The kittens spent hours batting the baubles till they fell off, or just gazing at the twinkling lights. How intriguing! Sometimes the lights didn't move but just reflected off the many baubles, at other times they flashed on and off or chased each other round the tree. It was all so mesmerising.

The great thing about the tree was there was so much to play with. All the decorations could be batted separately. Some of them made a nice tinkling sound and some rolled round the floor like a ball if you could knock them off. The ribbons and bows could be pulled and twisted and the reflection of the lights could be pounced upon. Oscar wanted to go a step further though. It seemed it was always Poppy who was the first to try new experiences, and where she led, he followed. The Christmas tree was going to be different. He was going to show off his climbing skills, so that for once she would have to copy him. The tree was mounted on a small table in front of the window in the living room and from Oscar's point of view, there were several possible angles of attack. Should he leap from ground level, two feet to the base of the tree, or should he jump from the television stand which he was still small enough to climb on? No, the most exciting, and indeed the most courageous route, would be to launch himself from the arm of the sofa, across the air for about three feet, and then dive straight into the tree, a few branches up from the base. Unfortunately, once he had made the leap and grabbed hold of the central trunk of the tree, he was stuck. If he let go he would fall into the lower branches, entangling himself in fairy lights and silver baubles. He could not climb higher for the same reason. Gravity came to his rescue and, in what seemed like slow motion, both Oscar and the tree lurched sideways and collapsed in a heap on the floor, decorations rolling in all directions. Tracey, Mike and I collapsed with laughter. Oscar, shell-shocked by the chaos surrounding him, scarpered and ran up the stairs. Poppy, skittish at the best of times, ran upstairs with him. You could imagine her rolling her eyes at him in disdain.

CHAPTER 2

GETTING TO KNOW EACH OTHER

This was the first Christmas Mike and I were going to spend together. We had started dating in October the previous year, but I had spent last Christmas in Devon with my sister and her family. Mike and I had met through the Internet, which at the time was not necessarily considered the ideal way to meet a partner. When I made the decision to sign up to a dating website, I was unsure if I should even mention that I had cats on my profile, but decided I should as they are important to me. When you start Internet dating, you very quickly learn what 'sells' and what does not. You also soon discover that many profiles are pretty much the same and lacking in imagination, as if they had followed some sort of banal template. Some cried out with bitterness, 'I'm looking for a woman who doesn't want to change me, like everyone else I've met.' Some were too good to be true, 'I'm American with a condo in Aspen, an apartment in Manhattan and a chateau in France, but still looking for that special lady. All ages/sizes considered.' Bizarrely, I seemed to be attracting a lot of elderly gentlemen from Cleethorpes. Not that I have anything against people from Cleethorpes, but living in Jersey it was hardly practical. Furthermore, I was not looking for a much older partner. I was in my early forties and looking for someone in a similar age bracket. Maybe I shouldn't have mentioned the cats.

Although some of my friends were sceptical

about my using a dating site, I had been single for a few months and wanted to be proactive in my search for a potential partner.

After a few unsuccessful encounters with over-familiar and frankly cringeworthy suitors, I had almost given up on the idea of Internet dating. However, I decided to give it one final go and it turned out to be a very good decision. I found Mike. I thought he looked lovely. Tall (unless his photograph was taken next to a very small door, which I suppose could have been a possibility), immaculate, wearing a dinner suit (which in my mind is the best look on a man), with dark hair and blue eyes that seemed to sparkle. He looked Just My Type.

I read his blurb. He had excellent written English. I am quite particular about things like that. He didn't mention that he 'enjoyed nights out' or was 'equally happy at home curled up on the sofa with a DVD and a glass of wine', which is the Internet equivalent of 'Do you come here often?' He said that he was divorced with two children (this was true), he said he was two years younger than me (this was true), he said he was 6 feet 2 inches tall (true, which is amazing as apparently, the most common lie people put about themselves on dating sites is about their height), that he liked going to the gym (this was true for a brief time) and enjoyed sailing (apparently true but in the six years I've known him, I've never seen any evidence of it). As I read through his profile, I thought he sounded funny and self-deprecating. I composed (what I thought to be) a witty, light-hearted email and sent it off. It was around 10.30 p.m. on Saturday night and I waited for the reply. I realised that he might be out, so was patient. No reply came. I checked again at midnight, in case he had been out. Nothing. It was Saturday so I could stay up a bit later. I checked again at 1.00 a.m.; OK, time for bed, I would check the next day. I got up early to see if there were any messages. Again, there was nothing. I re-read what I had sent. Did I sound too needy? Too hopeful? Too eager? I wasn't sure.

The following weekend when there was still no reply, I thought, 'Oh well, you win some, you lose some.' I was disappointed though, as he was the only person on the site based in Jersey who I liked the look and sound of. It seemed I would have to go further afield. I checked the site to see if any new people had joined. Sundays were quite a popular day for new recruits—presumably after their having had a miserable weekend. Whilst checking for suitors, an email popped up. Mike had finally replied! It was a lovely email, explaining he had been busy all week but that he liked the sound of me. As I was a cool customer, I thought I would wait another week before replying. But I couldn't. I was anything but cool. Mike could barely have pressed 'send' before I fired off my reply.

That is how it all started. We progressed from email to MSN Messenger on which one evening, we had a conversation that lasted from midnight to six in the morning. The next day we spoke on the phone and then, after a further sixty or so hours of online chatting, about a week later, we finally met in person. I was cautious about arrangements: we didn't meet for lunch, instead we met in a pub equidistant from both our houses; I suggested six o'clock, knowing that if it did not go well I could still walk home in daylight. We stayed until closing time, our conversation never faltering. Mike walked me home and we haven't looked back. The odd thing was how we had never met before. We had umpteen mutual connections, we worked in the same industry, we had similar tastes, and we lived less than a mile apart. Many people, including some of my closest friends, feel that Internet dating carries a stigma, but I don't subscribe to that point of view. For my part it was the best decision I ever made, and Mike and I are never bashful about how we met.

Even though it was important to me that I did not come across to Mike (or indeed anyone) as a forty-something, childless, crazy cat lover, it could not be denied that my two old cats were very important to me.

Mike and I had been together for a little over a year when Oscar and Poppy came into our lives. We lived separately and had a very contented, easy relationship. I had unwittingly become something that I had never anticipated, a single woman with two cats. The previous few years had been traumatic for me. I had split up with my long-term partner and had found myself single at forty with nowhere to live. Living in Jersey, but not having been born there, I had to 'serve my time' before I was able to buy property or rent in my own name due to Jersey's housing restrictions. At the beginning of the year I finally became 'residentially qualified' which enabled me to rent or buy freely (although the exorbitant house prices somewhat limited the choices). One of my main concerns was to find a place that would accommodate my cats, Berlioz (Buzz) and Toulouse (Lou). They are beautiful British Shorthair cats. Toulouse is lilac cream, which is grey with flecks of cream to you and me, and Berlioz is a tortoiseshell. Whilst they were from the same litter, their frame and temperaments were very different. They had been my companions for almost four years. My ex-partner and I had acquired them through a house we rented. The owner (of both the house and the cats—if cats can have owners that is), was relocating to Ireland and intended to re-house his cats somewhere in Jersey. When I asked if I could have them he readily agreed, warning me that they were 'a bit funny'. He wasn't wrong.

They had also been saddled with silly names—Berlioz and Toulouse. I had been told which cat was which, but somehow I had managed to confuse them, and for a few weeks they were called by the wrong names. Not that it mattered hugely, as they rarely responded to their names. Of course, if there was a whiff of chicken in the air, they would appear automatically. If I was calling them in for a tin of supermarket, own-brand, chicken-flavoured cat food ('flavoured' being the operative word), of course they wouldn't come. My mother had a theory that if you fed cats the cheapest make of cat food from the word go, they wouldn't know any different, so start as you mean to go on. Two points here. Firstly Berlioz and Toulouse were five years old and fairly discerning. Secondly, my mother is more of a dog person. Even so, I remembered too late to heed her advice with Oscar and Poppy.

'The Girls', as Berlioz and Toulouse became collectively known, did however display signs that their diet had been far from ideal. For a couple of the months, Colin (their previous owner), had relied on his father (a dour Scotsman) to feed the cats whilst he worked abroad.

'I give them the biscuits an' a tin o' the cat food each day,' he advised me, as he did the initial handover of the cats. 'They get reet under yer feet. I got no time for them, little rats. No idea why Colin bothers with them.' Although gruff and very disparaging about the cats, he did walk almost four miles every day to feed them and, in his own way, I think he was quite fond of them. Unfortunately, their lifestyle (do cats have lifestyles?) was having a poor effect on their health. British Shorthair cats have very dense fur that separates in rows; this is known as crisp or cracking fur, however to me it looks rather like the armoured back of an armadillo. Berlioz, who was the bigger of the two cats, had stubby little legs and a propensity to being overweight. Rather than being sleek and shiny, she produced an excessive amount of fur and her dull coat was covered in dandruff. Toulouse had a big sore under her neck where she had cut herself and her collar had been rubbing. I do not like cats wearing collars, as I think they find them an encumbrance that they cannot do anything about. When I removed her collar, it was evident that medical attention was needed and after a course of antibiotics, she was well on the way to recovery.

Bonding with them was a little trickier. Neither Berlioz nor Toulouse were comfortable being picked up. As soon as you swooped either of them up into your arms, they would wriggle until they could set themselves free and land back on the floor. They would not sit on your lap and were generally resistant to being touched. I put this down to the fact that either they had not been handled enough as kittens, or that they had been neglected and lacked human company as they got older. However, when I was browsing through a book in a library, I discovered that they were typical of their breed. I read that British Shorthairs are 'four paws on the floor' cats, and so it proved to be. Occasionally Toulouse would rub past my legs when a pouch of food was being opened, or Berlioz would lie next to me on the sofa, but they would never sit on you.

Gradually, over the following months, they became more used to me and would let me pick them up. I once held Toulouse for almost two minutes before she'd had enough. I did actually time it. One other thing I had to change was their names. I got really fed up telling people they were called Berlioz and Toulouse, 'but I didn't name them', so their names were contracted to Buzz and Lou, which was much easier. Also, most people thought Buzz was a male named after *Toy Story*'s Buzz Lightyear. Mind you, I had only just found out that Berlioz and Toulouse were kittens from Disney's film, *The Aristocats*.

The big turning point in my relationship with these diffident cats occurred well before I met Mike. It was the day I came back from a holiday in Thailand. I had left the cats at home, (rather than putting them in a cattery) and had a rota of friends who kindly came round and fed them, picking up the odd mouse along the way. One of my friends, Jacqui, was so traumatised at finding a dead mouse in the kitchen that, over ten years later, she still talks about it. As a cat owner who is used to seeing the spoils of your feline's hunting spree, it's easy to underestimate how such carnage can affect those unfamiliar with similar scenes.

After a gruelling fourteen hours in a crowded economy-class plane back from Bangkok, a five-hour wait at Gatwick and a further flight to Jersey, I was shattered by the time I got home. After I had had a proper cup of tea, I hit the sack. In the morning, following a deep sleep, I awoke to find both Buzz and Lou curled up on the bed, for the first time ever. They had missed me, it was obvious. I never once thought that it was the warmth of a human body that made the bed so appealing! It was January, after all.

And so life went on. Buzz and Lou were not the most active of cats, preferring to spend their days in the urban garden, or in the case of Lou, who was a real sun-worshipper, lying by the French windows as the sun streamed in. Lou's purring was strong and pronounced as she lay prone, having her tummy tickled. Buzz preferred her head being stroked and found any attempt at placing a hand near her abdomen to be a huge invasion of privacy and as such would lash out with her claws if your hand so much as hovered near her belly. Whilst undoubtedly pretty, with a round face and big round eyes, the roundness extended to her whole body. Her tummy was in danger of touching the floor, despite the fact she only seemed to pick at her food and wasn't greedy. This could well be where her heinous dislike of her sister came from. She was jealous. Lou was pretty, but she was also dainty and small. She had the bigger appetite but no weight problems. Maybe Buzz was unhappy about this, but whatever the real reason she took every opportunity to hiss at her sister, whether it was passing each other in the kitchen when Lou

23

got attention from the humans or when she jumped through the cat flap—whatever it was, Buzz would hiss and lash out at Lou. Buzz was definitely the sort of cat that would have been happiest being a solo feline with humans. It is a human belief that animals need company, but the domestic cat is very comfortable living without other cats around them and I was pretty sure Buzz would have preferred to be an only cat. This posed one of the major dilemmas a few years down the line when Mike and I were talking about bringing Oscar and Poppy into the household.

In short, my life changed considerably in the space of a few years. I had come from a relationship that had broken down, to earning my residential qualifications which, in turn, enabled me to buy an apartment in the countryside as a new home for me, Buzz and Lou. The apartment was in a converted barn and was surrounded by open countryside and I was sure the cats were going to love it as much as I did. It was strange at first. I had not been on my own for many years and initially having sole responsibility for a mortgage was onerous. It did not take me long to enjoy the advantages though. I bought some bright-pink glitter emulsion and painted the bathroom. It would have looked great had I not managed to get paint on the ceiling, the light fitting, the tiles on the floor, the taps. In fact, despite returning the wall to a more subtle cream shade a year or so later when the novelty wore off, remnants of the pink glitter paint remained in just about every nook and cranny. When I eventually sold my flat the first thing the purchasers did was rip out the bathroom. I bet the glitter paint lives on though.

Lou loved the sun that streamed through the huge windows in my lounge at the barn, and Buzz spent every night on the side of the bed where there had once been a man. It was a happy time for the three us, keeping each other company and pottering about. Despite Buzz's abject dislike of her sister, she really loved people. Not in the pick-me-up-and-cuddle-me way, more just lying in the same the room as them, listening to them talking.

For much of the time we also had a third cat in the flat. Moss lived next door to me and made his presence felt from the day I moved in. An enormous, pale marmalade British Shorthair with the most docile nature you could find in a cat. Untypical of his breed, he was more than happy to be picked up and it was almost like handling a rag doll, he just flopped in your arms. He was a very friendly neighbour. He often popped through the cat flap to check up on Buzz and Lou as they settled in after we moved there. He occasionally wandered into the lounge but his preferred place to sleep was on the rug in the hall. This did rather inconvenience Buzz and Lou if they wanted to use the cat flap, but in those early days they were not really sure if they were on Moss's territory or vice versa.

He was sure they did not mind sharing their Whiskas with him. He had a big girth he needed to maintain. Moss liked to share his love and it was common to visit one of the other neighbours and find him sitting in a cosy corner.

My flat was actually the first floor of the barn conversion with an exterior staircase leading to a veranda and front door. The three flats in the barn, along with three other houses, were laid out in a small close and we all knew each other well.

Moss's primary residence was a pretty cottage at the corner of the close which belonged to a couple that had decided to go travelling. They rented out their house to a young couple who had recently had a baby and whilst they were happy to rent it furnished, understandably did not want to take on a cat too.

One of the other neighbours, Sarah, agreed to take on Moss so he did not have to move very far, this arrangement only served to make Moss more free-roaming than ever. He found himself evicted from the house he had been used to getting his meals from for the past couple of years, but whilst mildly confused, he soon learned where feeding time might be at any one residence.

'Is Moss round at yours?' one neighbour would ask another.

'Yes, he's on the bed.'

'Ah OK, that's fine, I just hadn't seen him this morning.'

He was everything you would want from a cat: you could pick him up and he would purr gratefully, he would sleep on your lap, but he was still independent and led his life how and where he chose. When I eventually moved, I told the people that had bought my flat about the visiting cat, but I omitted to tell them his name. When I spoke to them a few months after they had moved in, they said he visited every day and they had named him 'Dave'. Now, despite my preference for non-human names, this, I thought, was an excellent moniker. After a year of travelling Moss's parents returned and I heard he had moved with them to the quayside village of St Aubin, about three miles away.

CHAPTER 3

THE MOVE

Meanwhile, as winter gave way to spring, over at Mike's house the kittens grew rapidly. They became easier to tell apart as Oscar's face became more masculine and had more pointy features, whilst Poppy, who was growing at a slower rate anyway, retained the round softness of her face. Oscar's coat became sleeker and less fluffy. By now Mike and I had made a major decision too; I was selling my flat and we were buying a home together.

Browsing through the Internet one evening, I saw a charming little house for sale in Grouville, a parish in the south-east part of Jersey. It looked ideal. It had three bedrooms (one for us and one for each of Mike's children), an open fireplace and above all, it was surrounded by fields. The picture showed a cute symmetrical cottage, looking just like the sort of house a child would draw, with windows on either side of the central front door that had flowers growing around it. The price too was within our budget. At the time the property market was going through the roof and finding an affordable house in a place like Jersey, which has some of the most expensive real estate in world, was no mean feat.

'I think I've found somewhere,' I said on the phone to Mike. 'It's only come on the market today. It needs modernisation, but it's really reasonable for what it looks like. Shall we go and view it tomorrow?' I knew we could not hang around.

'I can't tomorrow. I'm on a training day. Will you go on your own and let me know what you think?' he replied.

I emailed Mike the website link and he confirmed that it did indeed look like a potential property for us. We had viewed around twenty properties, but most of them lacked character, went to offer before we could put ours in or were in the wrong location. The fact that we would be a household of four cats definitely played a part in our decision-making process and we wanted to avoid being on a busy road.

The next day in my lunch hour I was at the cottage. The communal parking with the next-door neighbours did not seem ideal and the patio garden needed attention. The roof was missing slates and, worryingly, there were huge vertical cracks in the render on the gable end. The chimney stack was at an angle and looked as if it would fall off at the slightest gust of wind.

Even though the house had been built in approximately 1820, the decor was firmly in the 1980s. Inside was a long, narrow kitchen, all in white Formica and not the modern high-gloss style that was the prevailing fashion. The electric hob was built in to the worktop but there was no splashback or extractor hood. I had not seen a neon kitchen light for many years. Despite this, the room had character, leaded light windows and a rough, natural-textured wall, both of which added to the cottage feel of the room.

I walked through to the lounge and the focal point of the inglenook fireplace was wonderful. The large, hooded open fire sat in the middle of a raised plinth, which housed the logs. I could forgive the green flowery carpet, the Anaglypta wallpaper on the ceiling and the pink walls because the room had ceiling beams. Genuine, original beams. Bizarrely, the cupboard in the lounge housed the hot water tank and was being used as an airing cupboard. I walked up the creaking staircase into the bathroom and looked around in disbelief. It comprised a vintage bath (and not in a good way), a toilet and sink with painted roses on them (which were peeling away) and gold taps. The floor and walls were a mismatch of blue and white tiles and the radiator seemed to have been painted with blue textured paint. The walls of the bedrooms were covered in woodchip wallpaper in varying shades of peach and grey. Polystyrene tiles were stuck to the ceiling in all the upstairs rooms. Throughout the house, all the skirting boards, doors and frames were painted in gunmetal grey gloss. Ruched Austrian blinds and net curtains adorned the windows. It would cost a fortune to renovate. It would take forever. It was love at first sight.

As soon as I got back to my car, I tried to call Mike, but I couldn't get hold of him so texted him to call me urgently. I did not know if he would be able to contact me from his training course. I knew I had to act quickly. I made the call.

Later in the afternoon Mike managed to pop out from the hotel where he was learning, not for the first time in his life, the importance of customer care.

'Hi darling, I got your text. What was the house like?' he asked.

'It needs loads of work doing to it. It's falling apart. You'll die when you see the decor. I've made an offer for the full asking price,' I gushed.

'Have you really?' Mike asked, knowing it is the sort of thing I would do, but probably hoping for rather more consultation on such a major decision.

'Yes, I thought we'd better move fast with it. The cats will love it; there are fields all around it. You can go and see it tomorrow.'

'Have they accepted the offer?' said Mike, trying to digest all the information.

'They're going to call back later.'

Much to our relief, our offer was accepted and luckily for me, Mike loved the house too and could see the potential.

I got an offer on my flat straightaway from a delightful young couple, so it looked like we were in business. Until, that is, we had the survey done on the cottage. It was awful; page after page of things to do, from a new roof to new wiring, rendering, drainage and water supply. It went on and on. We knew that there was work to do, but receiving a twelve-page report detailing the essential repairs required put the matter into perspective. We advised our estate agent of the news and he relayed this to the vendors who, much to our surprise, and certainly very unusual in the prevailing market conditions, reduced the price by nearly 20 per cent. We were delighted, although we realised that this saving would be eaten up by the work we would have to do to bring the house up to modern standards.

Everything was back on track and we were due to move on 29 February 2008. It turned out to be a day full of portent. That morning I popped in to see my advocate at his offices to sign the final paperwork regarding the sale of my flat, but we were taken aback that the sale fell through at the very last moment. Further along the chain, one of the parties was not able to generate the money required and so nothing and no one moved.

Although we were shocked and in a state of disbelief, all four cats were equally bewildered in their respective homes. Buzz and Lou get fidgety every time the suitcases come down from the loft, so to be completely surrounded by packing boxes was unsettling to say the least. They walked around and sniffed them. They peered in, but their curiosity did little to hide their anxiety as they paced from room to room clearly wondering what was about to happen. The kittens meanwhile were rather enjoying being surrounded by boxes. For them they had been given an amazing adventure playground. They clambered into the boxes and lay on the books stored inside. They nestled down in the box full of bed linen. They leapt from box to box with the agility of urban street runners. If this is what moving house was about they were all for it.

On that Friday none of us knew that we would have to live amongst the packing boxes for a further month. Luckily the chain was effectively reconnected (with new purchasers) and despite property transactions only taking place on Fridays, in hindsight, only having to wait four more weeks was very speedy.

Mike and I sat in the Royal Court, where property transactions take place every Friday, waiting nervously for something to go awry, but this time, all was well. All the sales in the chain went through and we finally had our own little cottage!

Mike and I had agreed that we would move all the things from my flat first and let Buzz and Lou

31

settle in. Although Mike would live at the cottage, the kittens, along with his furniture, would stay put until Tracey moved into her new flat in a couple of weeks' time.

Whilst our new cottage was everything we could have hoped for, there was one disadvantage that we had not fully appreciated when we viewed it. The road outside, it transpired, was a rat run for commuters and became busy with traffic at peak times. We had viewed the cottage four times in total, but each time it was around lunchtime on a weekday, which as it happened was the quietest time apart from late at night. My flat on the other hand, had been set back from the road, thus meaning that Buzz and Lou were a few years out of practice in dealing with traffic.

Nonetheless the cats adapted well to their new home. Buzz was happy as long as there were humans around. The new environment did not improve her temperament, though. She was turning into a cantankerous grande dame. Lou only had to walk past to cause a witch-like hiss from her. For no apparent reason, she would strike Lou with her paw. Lou, so used to this constant bullying, took it in her stride and walked away. She never lashed back; instead she let her bigger, grumpier sister have her own way.

Despite her terrible behaviour, Buzz was the most loving of the cats to humans. Every night she would climb on the bed and snuggle up. She was affectionate and rewarded you with pneumatic purring just for lying next to her. She was a people's cat for sure.

Whilst the cats got used to their new surroundings, Mike and I busied ourselves finding homes for everything in the dilapidated cupboards and skew-whiff shelves. We wrote list after list of jobs to do around the house, starting with the essentials like a waterproof roof and new rendering. We would think about a new kitchen and bathroom later.

A few weeks after we had moved in, I heard a strange meow coming from Mike's son Chris's room. I went to investigate. Chris, in typical teenage-boy style, had left the wardrobe door wide open, and there in the base was Buzz curled up in the corner.

'Are you all right?' I asked, trying to stroke her. She seemed to be crying in pain. I gently reached to pick her up and move her to the bedroom floor but she could barely stand up. I quickly looked her over and whilst there was no obvious sign of injury, something was clearly amiss. We rang the vet's and made an urgent appointment. Poor thing, even getting her into the cat box seemed to be causing her major discomfort.

We explained to the vet the circumstances of finding her and how we had only just moved.

'I'd say she's been hit by car,' she said as she felt round Buzz's flanks. 'I don't think anything is broken but I'd like to X-ray her just to be on the safe side.'

We waited in the reception area until Buzz had been seen to and then the vet called us back in to the consulting room.

'There don't appear to be any broken bones. She's probably very badly bruised, so I'm going to prescribe some medication and it's best if you keep her in for a while,' she explained. To my knowledge Buzz had never had an accident before and it seemed ironic for her to have her first one when we had only just moved to our idyllic country cottage.

Of course if experienced, mature Buzz could have an encounter with a car, what did this mean for the two flighty kittens? If only we had known that Buzz's visit to the vet was a prelude to many, many further visits with Oscar.

Buzz recovered well but a week or so later, Mike and I were sitting at the kitchen table drinking coffee, when I sensed tension from Mike.

'Are you OK?' I asked, thinking that he was about to say it had all been a terrible mistake and we should never have moved in together.

'It's the kittens,' he replied, stirring his drink slowly and not looking at me.

'How can we bring them here with Buzz and Lou and the traffic?' he continued.

In my mind he had good reason to be worried. Oscar and Poppy were both still half fully grown and the thought of bringing them into such a potentially hostile environment was concerning.

'I know. Buzz'll probably kill them,' I said, not really sure if I was joking or not.

'We could have Buzz rehomed,' I was definitely joking this time. At that moment she wandered into the kitchen and rubbed her rotund body and stubby legs around me. 'Don't listen to Mummy, Buzz. I want you to be a nice girl to your new brother and sister,' I continued stroking her head and was rewarded by loud purring.

'Look at her,' said Mike, 'butter wouldn't melt. I guess as long as the others respect her position of alpha cat, it should be OK. We'll just have to wait and see. I'm not looking forward to it though.'

Neither was I. At my previous flat when Moss

started to pop through the cat flap and sleep in the hall, after some initial reticence when we first moved in, Buzz defended her territory fiercely. 'No squatters here!' she'd seem to screech as she hissed at the intruder. He was not deterred by Buzz. Despite her shooing him away almost every day for two years, he continued to visit. Other cats in the vicinity, however, feared her wrath and one encounter with her was enough to make them scarper for good.

We researched how to integrate new cats into a family, but when the day came we were both filled with trepidation. I had read that sometimes you never could integrate cats if there is too much hostility. I feared the worst.

The day finally arrived; Mike brought the cat carrier into the lounge and put it on the green swirly eighties-style carpet. Buzz and Lou were lounging on the two sofas unaware that their lives were about to change for good. They both woke with a start when they heard the mews from the kittens.

Buzz was the first to investigate and, as predicted, she was not happy. She went to the grille at the front of the carrier as the poor little kittens cowered at the back of the box. She hissed with all her might. Lou was behind her, curious and furious at these imposters in the house.

'This is totally normal behaviour,' I reassured Mike as Buzz tried to poke her paw through the plastic at the front of the box.

The kittens were crying, huddling up to each other for comfort, having retreated to the back of the box. Surprisingly, after some initial curiosity, Lou walked away and jumped back onto the sofa.

Buzz, on the other hand, needed to get these creatures expelled from her territory as quickly as possible. She hissed and spat and patrolled around the box as if she were trapping her prey. She pulled herself on top of the box and peered in through the air vents on the side of it. I tried to lift her away but she lashed out at me and drew blood.

'I think that's enough for today,' Mike said taking the terrified kittens to the safety of the bedroom which would be their home until integration was complete.

Each day we allowed Oscar and Poppy to explore more of the house, whilst we shut Buzz and Lou in another room. They climbed and sniffed and scratched and played. They seemed tiny in comparison to the other two and it was delightful to see them exhibiting their kittenish behaviour. We knew it would not be long before they were all grown up.

Buzz in particular was very curious about the kittens. When they were locked in the bedroom, Buzz would listen to them playing and as they became more settled, heard them scratching at the door. Buzz would scratch back, hoping to be granted a visitor's pass no doubt. She was out of luck. We exchanged toys so that Buzz and Lou could smell the kittens and vice versa. Unsurprisingly, Buzz and Lou were not great fans of toys. Every year I had wasted money buying them Christmas and birthday felt mice or plastic 'fishing rods' with feathers on the end. They were never the slightest bit interested. I could almost hear them saying to me, 'And why would I want a PRETEND mouse?' like a surly teenager.

To get their scent on the toys, we had to rub

them in the cats' fur. This, I think they thought, was probably the best use for these rather pointless objects. At least it was a nice back rub.

Gradually the face-to-face meetings with the kittens were reintroduced. We supervised carefully to ensure there was no blood on the carpet. Buzz calmed down and her extreme hostility was replaced with inquisitiveness. She sniffed the little furry creatures and they sniffed her back. She did not try to scratch them unless their hyperactivity caught her off guard. She watched, almost with admiration, as with increasing confidence, they raced round the lounge, leaping from chair to table to sofa as they went. She tolerated them charging up and down the stairs and though not tempted to join in with the shenanigans, she did not display her normal angry-at-everything characteristics.

Everyone settled into a new routine. Instead of two sittings for mealtimes, all four ate in a row. Buzz and Lou were delighted to have a new father figure in the house in the form of Mike as, unlike their mother, he cooked fresh fish or chicken for the little darlings every night.

Poppy and Oscar were desperate to go outside, but we decided to follow conventional wisdom and wait until they had been settled for three weeks. Following Buzz's accident we were extra wary and in the meantime we had also had to take Lou to the vet's, as she had come home one day unable to walk. The vet seemed to think she might have been bitten by a rat or possibly another cat in a fight. We did not think Lou was the sort of cat to get into a fight. Her routine consisted of sunbathing, sleeping and eating, but we conceded we did not know what went on outside when we weren't around, particularly at night. We occasionally heard screeching and hissing but put it down to tomcats from the nearby farm. There are no foxes in Jersey, so we knew it was not that. Maybe Lou was asserting herself in her new territory—we would never be sure.

So, for these reasons, we wanted to be careful before we let the little ones experience the great outdoors again. As we should have guessed, the kittens had other ideas. We made the schoolboy error of leaving the kitchen window open and within moments of a fresh air wafting past Poppy's nose, she was off. If a soundtrack had been playing, it would have been the music to *The Great Escape*. She leapt onto the kitchen table, across on to the windowsill, then up to the top window and she was gone. Oscar, not wanting to miss out on fun, was hot on her paws. They ran across the courtyard to the garden, overwhelmed by all the new smells of the countryside. They had been townies before, so this was a whole new world to them. They scaled the trellis like two monkeys and carefully balanced themselves as they walked across the wall that separated our garden from the field. They jumped on to the roof of the neighbouring old barns and roamed in the abundant honeysuckle.

'Come down you two!' I pleaded with them as they looked down at me and of course totally ignored me. They were having far too much fun to pay any attention.

As each day passed and spring turned to summer, they spent more and more time outdoors. We watched them gingerly cross the road to the big field opposite us. The Jersey cows that were there when we first moved in had gone and been replaced with crops. Oscar and Poppy loved it over there, running along looking for the mice which had made their home in the plants. The kittens started to go their separate ways. Oscar was more of a homebody, never liking to be away from his food bowl for more than an hour or two, whereas Poppy disappeared for hours on end, returning home only at the end of a long, exhausting day. Poppy was still very small for her age and stopped growing long before Oscar it seemed.

The dynamics of the four cats continued to develop and change. Oscar suffered a similar fate to a lot of boys living in a family of females; he was outclassed, overruled and pushed out of the way by his siblings. His large, majestic frame, sleek black coat and extremely long tail disguised the fact that he was on the lowest rung in the pecking order. At mealtimes the girls would nudge Oscar out of the way if he was still chomping and they had finished. Poppy and Lou dominated the sofa whilst Buzz favoured the warm spot by the radiator. Oscar ended up on the rather more uncomfortable spot of the computer chair.

Whilst the cats were establishing their status, including the development of rather unexpected mutual respect between Poppy and Buzz ('I want to be like you when I grow up, you're so cool!') Mike and I got on with DIY. Our receipts mounted up as we bought endless bits and pieces to stop the house from falling down. I developed a mild addiction to the smell of paint stripper as I spent hours bringing a granite lintel back to its original state, removing layer upon layer of emulsion. Mike concentrated on the practicalities and spent several weekends insulating the loft and laying a floor. At least I think that is what he was doing; I never ventured up there.

CHAPTER 4

The Christmas Tree and The Car

By the time December arrived we were pleased that we were making headway with the house and we had adjusted to living together with ease. Of course we could not agree on all decisions, but there was one I was determined to win.

'It's way too early,' answered Mike when I suggested we get the Christmas tree.

'No, it's not. If we leave it too late all the nice trees will have gone,' I retorted.

That was not the real reason; I just loved Christmas. Everyone seemed to have a spring in their step as the evenings got darker and the houses started to twinkle with coloured lights. I loved the baking, getting all the red and green recipe books off the shelf and making far too much food. I spent hours poring over various food magazines, which I added to each year, although the recipes were all pretty similar, just photographed slightly differently or styled in that year's colour of choice. There was always a 'perfect roast turkey' recipe, a chocolate Yule log, a decorated cake, a gingerbread house and mince pie recipes. It didn't matter to me that I probably had twenty different recipes for chestnut stuffing that I never used, due to the widely accepted preference for Paxo Sage & Onion. It was just the ritual of getting a new Christmas food magazine.

'If we get the tree now, the needles will have dropped off by Christmas,' countered Mike.

'Shall we have a look at some anyway just to get an idea?' I asked.

'I know what they look like! OK, let's have a look when we're out.'

Mike was such a softy. I didn't think putting up decorations in the first week or so of December was unreasonable, and I agreed with Mike when he said that as children we did not decorate until we broke up from school around 20 December. However, Christmas seems more of a month-long event these days or considerably longer if you are a retailer.

We went to the garden centre and sized up the tree. There were so many to choose from it was all very confusing. Being our first Christmas in the cottage, we were not entirely sure what size tree would look right in the lounge. But in the end, we selected what we hoped would be the perfect one to hold all of our decorations.

On the way home we stopped off in St Helier to go to the one shop that to me, totally epitomised Christmas.

We walked though aisles of chocolates and sweets and continued past wrapping paper, ribbon and greetings cards for every member of the family. We passed DVDs and CDs and endless computer games. It was still early enough in December for the background music of 'Merry Christmas Everyone' to be exciting and fresh.

The Christmas decorations area filled the space that was usually occupied with haberdashery and laundry goods. Rows and rows of tinsel in blue, purple, green, silver, gold, red and even black, hung beside endless types of fairy lights with blue lights making a surprise appearance after years of domination by white lights. Our humble pack of replacement lights looked insignificant amongst all the garish splendour, but we bought them, knowing how essential they could prove to be. We left the wonder of Woolworths and headed home to unload the tree. When we put it in front of the French door its girth, rather like our own, was rather broader than we hoped.

'We might have to trim the branches,' I suggested, as it seemed to span so much of the floor it was difficult to get to the dining table.

'Yes, and stick them on the top!' replied Mike. He was right, it was rather short. We decided to let the branches settle into position before taking any drastic action and went into the kitchen to have a cup of coffee. The light was starting to fade although it was only just past four o'clock.

'It's been such fun today,' I said.

'It's been great,' Mike agreed. 'I'll get the decorations down in a minute.'

A warm feeling spread through me as I anticipated our first Christmas together in our cosy cottage. We heard the cat flap swing open in the hall.

'Here's someone after food,' said Mike as he sipped his coffee. I turned round to see Oscar in the hallway. With an arched back, he was standing still, crying.

'Oh my God, is he all right?' I exclaimed, running into the hall. I crouched down and looked at his face. I could not see any obvious injuries. Then a big drop of blood dropped on the hall floor from his back end, then another and another. Then I saw his rear right leg was ripped open. Mike saw it too and grabbed the phone book without hesitation. He raced through the pages until he found the number for the vet's which he quickly tapped into the phone.

'*We are currently closed. Our opening hours for surgery are . . .*' said the recorded message.

'Come on,' urged Mike.

'*If you have an emergency please call . . .*' Mike dialled the number and the duty vet answered almost immediately.

'If you take him down to the animal hospital I'll be there in about twenty minutes.'

That was the very first contact we had with the vet who was about to start Oscar's remarkable medical journey with us.

I retrieved the cat carrier from the shed. It was covered in leaves and cobwebs so I gave it a quick rinse with the garden hose, dried it off and we carefully put Oscar onto a towel in the box. He meowed quietly and cooperated as we made him comfortable.

New Era Veterinary Hospital is only a short car journey from our house and we arrived before the vet. A duty nurse let us in through the side door and as we took a seat in the large, empty waiting room, a black and white cat stretched in a basket on top of the reception desk.

'You wouldn't expect to see that in a waiting room!' commented Mike.

'Maybe he just stays here at night,' I pondered, as the cat, who had completely ignored our presence, settled back down. Our wait was over in a matter of minutes and the vet invited us through to one of the consulting rooms.

He took Oscar out of his box and examined him whilst asking us if we had any idea what had happened, which we did not.

'He doesn't appear to have broken anything,' observed the vet, who we now knew was called Peter Haworth, a friendly man in his thirties.

'He may have been dragged along by a car,' he explained as he showed us Oscar's ripped claws on his front paws. 'I'd like to make him comfortable and take some X-rays. We'll keep him in tonight.'

Poor old Oscar, we thought. At least he is in the best place. Peter went through the formalities with us, checking our names, address and Oscar's details.

'Are you insured?' he asked.

'No, we're not,' replied Mike. No private room and à la carte menu for Oscar then.

We went home, with Peter promising to call later to update us on the situation. For the first time in my life, the thought of decorating the Christmas tree left me cold. Mike dragged the decorations down from the loft and I perfunctorily tossed them on to the branches. The wonder of unwrapping the fragile baubles and getting reacquainted with them was normally such a delight. This year it was just a chore. I could not be bothered to take the usual ornaments down from the mantelpiece and replace them with a festive scene.

'That looks nice,' Mike said, as he came in to witness the switching on of the lights. I knew he meant it, but the Christmas spirit we had relished earlier in the day had all but evaporated.

Later Buzz, Lou and Poppy all appeared in the kitchen as soon as they smelled their fish cooking. Lou shook her tail out like Basil Brush in her usual manner. Buzz and Poppy had a good sniff at each other to try and work out how they had each spent their day. Oscar's absence at a mealtime did not appear to have registered with any of them. As long as they each had their portion of haddock, all was fine.

Peter rang us mid-evening to confirm the good news that Oscar did not have any broken bones and that he had stitched up the wound on his leg and given him something to make him comfortable. He said they wanted to keep an eye on him overnight and that he would call again tomorrow.

We remarked to each other how lucky it was we were home when Oscar brought himself through the cat flap. If it had been a weekday we would not have been home from work until an hour and a half later. Thank goodness for that, we thought.

We spent a quiet Sunday pottering about waiting for the vet to call so we could find out how Oscar was doing. Later in the day the nurse rang to tell us Oscar was fine. 'He's comfortable. We're just waiting for him to pass urine, which he hasn't done yet. Peter reckons he should be home with you on Tuesday.' Our spirits lifted and we decided to go for a walk down the country lanes near our house. Outside the front door there was a trail of blood. We followed it in front of the house to the end of the road and round the corner. Poor Oscar had walked at least fifty or so metres from where the accident must have happened to get himself home.

On the way to work on Monday, Mike and I commented on what a strange weekend it had been: on the one hand, really exciting and Christmassy; on the other, so sad with Oscar's accident. It really had been a weekend of two halves.

I had not been at my desk for more than twenty minutes, when Mike called. My mood changed instantly. He would never call so early unless there was something major to report.

'We've got to make a decision. Peter's called and Oscar's in trouble,' Mike asserted without any introductory pleasantries. 'He's split his urcthra and they need to operate. The thing is it will cost £2,000.'

'Oh no! What will happen if they don't operate?' I asked, trying to take in the enormity of it all.

'Then they'll have to put him down, I'm afraid. The thing is they need to know straightaway as there isn't much time left for him,' Mike replied.

'Well, of course we'll go ahead,' I said to Mike.

Whether people thought we did the right thing by agreeing to pay out so much money was debatable. Certainly it was a huge amount of money to pay for our moggy, especially when we still needed so much doing to the house. At the same time we could not have imagined any other decision. Money did not come into it and we could worry about that later. All we knew is that we wanted to give Oscar a chance. I have since learnt from someone who was completing a stint of work experience at a veterinary practice, that some of the most challenging times for vets are when an animal can be saved because the medical procedures are available, but the owners just do not have the funds, so the animal has to be put down. That sort of situation must be so awful for all concerned. I am very grateful that Mike and I were able to afford to make this decision, albeit if we had to make the repayments over several months.

'Will the operation definitely work?' I asked.

'I'm not sure, but it's got to be worth a try,' Mike said before putting the phone down so that he could call the vet to advise them of our decision.

Both Mike and I spent our working day going through the motions until we received a call to say the operation had gone as well as could be expected and we were advised that we could visit Oscar that evening.

New Era Veterinary Hospital felt very different when it was actually open. Dogs of all sizes sat with their owners in reception. Cats cried from their boxes, some scared and uncomfortable at being in such close proximity to the dogs or, more likely, simply from grumpiness at the audacity of their owners for putting them in the box in the first place. Replacing the silence of our first visit was a general hubbub as the two girls on the desk were busy checking patients in, taking payments, booking appointments and generally making a fuss of the animals.

We were taken through to see Oscar who was in the kennels at the back. The cages were stacked up on top of each other and Oscar's was at eye level. He was sleepy and attached to a drip. He looked up and let out a little cry.

'Hello, Oscar. What have you done, you poor old thing?' I said as I looked at him looking dolefully at me.

The nurse, Amanda, opened the front of his cage so we could stroke him, taking care that we didn't knock his drip or catheter.

'He's doing OK,' explained Amanda. 'He's eaten quite well, he's had some chicken.'

Peter came through and explained what had happened.

'Basically the reason he wasn't passing urine was because his urethra was split open. The urine was leaking into his body, that's why we had to act fast. Unfortunately we've had to amputate his penis and make a new opening for his urethra, so effectively he'll pee like a girl in future.'

'Did the operation go OK?' asked Mike.

'It did,' said Peter, 'but it's still early days and, to be honest, a bit touch and go. I just want to see what happens to his skin over the next few days because I'm a bit worried about the urine seeping into the flesh. The urine is toxic and with prolonged contact will cause the flesh to die. We need to keep a close eye on everything to make sure that doesn't happen. Nonetheless, he's a young boy and he's got a lot of determination, so we're all rooting for him. With any luck, he'll be home in a few days.'

Whilst we were there, we had a look at the other cats in the neighbouring kennels, several of whom were victims of traffic accidents.

'There are a lot of black cats,' I remarked.

'Yes,' agreed one of the nurses, 'they are more prone to traffic accidents as they just don't get seen. Whatever you do, don't get a black cat and call it Lucky!'

Oscar had been lucky, but little did we know that he'd need a lot more than luck over the coming weeks and months.

The myths and legends surrounding black cats are fascinating and whether you believe black cats to be lucky or unlucky, depends largely on where you live. In Great Britain and Ireland they are considered to bring good luck. Scottish people think a black cat's arrival at your house brings prosperity, but in a great deal of Western history, black cats symbolise evil omens. In the Middle Ages in Germany it was believed that if a black cat jumped on the bed of a sick person, then that person would die. People at Steere House Rehabilitation Center in Rhode Island may well agree, although their Oscar isn't black. In Finland, black cats were believed to carry the souls of the dead to the afterlife and generally, black cats have played a large part in folklore and mythology and have long been associated with witchcraft. During the time of the bubonic plague, cats were thought to spread the disease and were rounded up and killed and this had the knock-on effect of exacerbating the spread of the plague due to the rat population not being effectively controlled. Some cat adoption centres in the USA refuse to allow black cats to be rehomed around Halloween for fear they may be tortured or used as living decorations in displays. In eighteenth- and nineteenth-century England, fishermen's wives kept black cats because they believed this helped to keep their husbands safe at sea and cats were also carried on ships to keep rats and mice at bay. If a black cat was thrown, or accidentally fell overboard, this was believed to bring bad luck in the form of a terrible storm.

Cats Protection (formerly The Cats Protection League, founded in 1927) said that nearly half the unwanted cats in their care were either black, or black and white and that they were much harder to find homes for. Whether people are favouring cats of other colours for superstitious or aesthetic reasons is arguable, but the sad fact is that black cats are not popular.

We left poor Oscar in the care of New Era Veterinary Hospital and hoped he would be home with us after a couple of days. On returning at visiting time the next day, we were told by the nurse that Peter wanted to see us.

'I'm sorry to say, but there have been some complications,' he gravely said. 'As I feared, the urine leaked below the skin and unfortunately the skin is starting to die. What we really need to do is a skin graft,' he explained.

Wow, this was quite a lot to take in. On Sunday we thought he would be home by Tuesday and now it was Tuesday and we are talking about more major surgery.

'The thing is though,' continued Peter, 'there is no guarantee that this will work. With skin grafts, sometimes they take and sometimes they don't.'

'What's his long-term prognosis?' asked Mike.

'Well, if it all goes well, then in six months' time Oscar could be totally back to normal. He's young and fit so hopefully he'll be running around fine. On the other hand if it doesn't work . . .'

Peter did not have to say any more. We agreed that he would proceed with the skin graft. It was going to be another £2,000. It was a huge amount of money, only affordable because we were able to pay back over several months.

The day after the operation we went to see Oscar and we were shocked at what we saw. He had been shaved from his waist, all over his back and tummy and down both back legs. He looked like the skinned rabbits you see in the market or at the butcher's; around the top of his hips he was being held together with staples. Worst of all, he had to wear a cumbersome 'Elizabethan collar' to prevent him from licking his wounds. This can be particularly distressing for cats as it also prevents them from grooming. It also affects their peripheral vision, but as Oscar was not moving very far, this was not the main concern. He was in a very sorry state, but somehow managed to muster up a purr when we stroked him.

'He's such a lovely little cat,' said Amanda, the nurse. 'He doesn't growl at all when we treat him. It's as though he knows we're trying to help him.'

The first week after the skin graft was a waiting game. It was still too early to say whether it had been a success or not. We visited daily, each time taking Oscar a little treat. His appetite had not diminished at all.

'He probably won't want to come home the food's so good here!' I said to Mike. The 'patients' had a diet of freshly cooked chicken, fish and tuna, so it was no wonder they all looked so comfortable.

About ten days after the operation, Peter gave us the good news that the graft seemed to be taking and the tissue was starting to granulate, which means the necessary beefy red tissue was developing as the wound started to heal. It looked very sore, but Peter assured us that it was not causing Oscar any pain at all.

Each time we had visited Oscar he had been in his cage, which sounds worse than it was. Inside there was a comfortable bed, a litter tray, food, water and toys, including Oscar's first, knitted, catnip-filled hedgehog. On this occasion we were allowed to take him out and let him have a walk around the consulting room and sit with him on our laps. He looked perfect from the front, his eyes were bright and his black furry face was as cute as ever. The rear was a different story; his fur had started to grow back so it was black and downy. His

51

tail had not come away from the accident unscathed and had a big chunk of fur missing about halfway down. He was stapled and stitched together like a much-loved but much-used old teddy. Despite this, he seemed quite perky. He walked around the floor and under the desk having a good sniff of all the furniture. A vet's consulting room must carry such an array of scents undetectable to the human nose, but fascinating for a cat whose sense of smell is about fourteen times better than a human's. As we watched him explore, we noticed he was starting to drip blood from underneath one of the staples.

'Oh my God, he's coming undone!' I exclaimed.

'Don't panic. I'll get someone,' Mike said, heading for the door.

'Sit still!' I commanded Oscar, momentarily forgetting he was not a dog. He continued to stroll around the room, unperturbed by the blood that was dribbling out of him and onto the floor at a pretty steady rate.

One of the nurses came in and picked Oscar up, giving him a quick once-over.

'Don't worry, it's just a small tear. We'll soon sort him out,' she assured us, taking him through to the back of the practice.

'It's quite stressful isn't it?' I said to Mike.

'It's fine. You worry too much. They know what they're doing.' He was absolutely right of course and after a few judicious stitches in the careful hands of Peter, Oscar continued to recover.

As we left that day, we stroked the black and white cat in the basket on the reception desk. We had learnt that her name was Jess and she used to live on the housing estate opposite the practice, but had crossed the busy main road and made herself at home and effectively moved in. She was completely unfazed by the comings and goings of the cats and dogs and other animals that came in for treatment. She was usually curled up asleep in her basket or occasionally wandering around. She was the perfect mascot for such a friendly vet practice.

Meanwhile Christmas was fast approaching. We had sent our cards out really late, what with all the worry about Oscar, and were frantically shopping for family and friends. I finally got round to putting the rest of the decorations up and eventually began to get into the spirit of the season. We received great news just before Christmas, when Peter said we could take Oscar home for a few days. He said he wanted him to be back at the surgery over Christmas itself, as it would be better for him to have a quiet environment, rather than be amidst all the commotion associated with the festivities.

It was a thrill to take Oscar home with us and we were sure that Buzz and Lou and, in particular, Poppy would have missed him.

We carefully drove him home, took him into the cottage and let him out of the cat carrier. He walked gingerly round the lounge, reacquainting himself with the home he had not seen for three weeks, but seemed a little hesitant and not sure of what to make of his new surroundings. Unfortunately, the Elizabethan collar (or 'buster collar' as the nurses had called it) he still had to wear was clearly a hindrance as he bumbled and bumped his way round the lounge with his head held low. Buzz and Lou showed only mild curiosity and gave him a cursory sniff. Poppy was initially hostile. This cat may have looked like her brother, but he sure as heck did not smell like him. He smelled slightly different to us, but Poppy's strong sense of smell meant she could not bear to get close to him. His time at the vet meant he had acquired an unfamiliar odour and it would take a few days before it faded.

Having Oscar home was great, but he was clearly not better and we had to administer pain relief every day. Fortunately this was in liquid form which we could mix into his food, knowing there was no way he would miss a meal, regardless of whether it had medicine in it or not. We also had to bathe his wound with a salt-water solution which was about the size of a chicken fillet on the inside of his thigh. His temperament remained as quiet and gentle as a teddy bear. Mike held Oscar in his arms whilst I dabbed the wounded area. Oscar did not once flinch, growl or hiss; he just took it all in his stride. We had never known a more malleable and calm cat.

Reluctantly, we took Oscar back to vet on Christmas Eve. He tried to hide when he saw the cat carrier in the kitchen, but he was under strict doctor's orders to return. When we got to the practice, most of the other patients had been discharged and Oscar was the only cat 'booked in' to be there over Christmas.

We went to visit him on Christmas Day, armed with a tin of chocolates for the staff and some turkey for Oscar.

'He's already had some king prawns,' informed Sarah, the duty nurse. All right for some, we thought. Unfortunately for Oscar his spell in the hospital would be a little longer than was strictly necessary as Mike and I were going on holiday immediately after Christmas to attend the wedding of two of our friends who were getting married abroad. Tracey had kindly agreed to come and house-sit for the other three cats, but with Oscar still in the throes of recovery it was considered best if he remained under medical supervision, just in case he needed further attention. We felt bad leaving him there but knew it was in his best interests and we were comforted by the thought that Tracey would be visiting him too. Mind you, he got so much love and affection from the staff at New Era, that he probably had no qualms about being there anyway.

At the beginning of January, Mike and I returned from our trip and could not wait to see Oscar. Kerry, the Head Nurse, took us through to one of the larger kennels, which Oscar had been transferred to. She was particularly fond of Oscar and took great delight in telling us how well he had been doing. We walked in to see him and he meowed, his tail went up and he came trotting towards us. We were delighted to see he was no longer wearing the collar. He rubbed his body back and forth along the metal grille and seemed as pleased to see us as we were to see him. Kerry told us that whilst his recovery had been excellent, we would need to continue with the pain relief and the salt baths. Finally, some six weeks after he had dragged himself through the cat flap on that December afternoon, Oscar was home for good. Or so we thought.

We developed a new routine at home. Oscar lived in the lounge with the door shut. He had his litter tray (occasionally used by Lou if she could not be bothered to go out), food, water and a bed. Of all the things Mike and I have wasted money on over the past few years, the biggest must be cat beds and at the last count we had seven in assorted shapes and sizes. They've all been put in the loft because all our cats end up on the human beds and human sofas and occasionally the human dining chairs (being leather they double as good scratching posts too). Oscar's sleeping place of choice was a corner of the sofa next to the log fire. One evening, when he had been back for around a week, Poppy surprised us all by jumping up next to him and lying down. She was starting to get used to him again.

Whilst we continued to nurse Oscar, builders started to work on the house. Scaffolding was erected so the crooked chimney and the roof could be replaced and the plasterers were booked to come later in the year to render the gable-end of the house. As someone once said, 'Always start with the envelope before you write the letter.' If it had been left to me I would have written the letter and decorated and fitted a new kitchen and bathroom, but Mike was far more sensible about the order in which we should renovate. Although the builders were only working on the outside of the house, we gave them access to the inside so that they could use the bathroom and kitchen. We kept the lounge door shut and put up a notice saying 'Sick cat inside, Keep Closed' so Oscar would not be let out inadvertently. He was still young and had a real spirit about him and we were well aware that if he got the opportunity to go out he would jump at the chance.

CHAPTER 5

A Spring in His Step

By the time March arrived, Oscar was allowed to go outside once again. We were naturally rather apprehensive about this, but thought it was part of his recovery for him to be allowed to return to normal life. He still looked a bit knocked about and although his fur was growing back, he looked like a patchwork quilt. The site of his wound, although much smaller, still appeared as pink raw skin about five inches in length and three inches in breadth. Peter advised us to put a collar on Oscar with a barrel on it, containing a note saying that he was currently undergoing medical treatment, together with a number to call. Mike and I are not in favour of cats wearing collars, not so much from the point of view of them getting caught in trees, as many collars will snap off should this happen; it was more that we both felt it was unnatural for cats to wear them and that they may be a source of irritation. I particularly dislike collars with bells; I appreciate they are there as a warning to birds, but I have always thought they must be really annoying to the cat. Nonetheless, in this instance it was obvious why putting a collar on Oscar would be prudent. We chose a nice reflective blue one, now he was pretty non-gender specific (now all his male parts had been removed!) and we wanted to make sure he was not emasculated too much. In his usual manner he let us attach the collar and metal barrel without fuss. He did not try to shake it off or use his paws to remove it. As with the veterinary treatment, it was as if he knew it was for his own good.

Initially we just let him out in the garden under supervision. He loved the freedom of being able to sniff around at leisure and as winter melted away, he would sit down and rest in the weak sun. Daffodils and crocuses emerged from the warming earth, followed by tulips and alliums, all of which heralded hope and optimism for the year ahead. Oscar did not try to wander too far or to jump, so little by little we let him out for longer until he was coming and going as he pleased. His acute hearing meant that as soon as the feeding bowls were put on the kitchen worktop in readiness for the next meal, he was through the cat flap at such a rate you would think there was an Alsatian running after him. We knew how to get him in if we thought he had been out for too long.

We were still busy working on the house and one of the things we were really keen to change was our water supply. We were on borehole water, which we had had analysed when we moved in. Whilst it was safe, the analysis had shown that it had almost three times the amount of nitrates recommended by the EU, and as a result we only drank bottled water, which, though not too expensive, was still rather a chore. Furthermore, the water turned my blonde highlights a rather unattractive shade of green, so I had my hair dyed back to my natural dark brown, which Mike preferred but I was less keen on. There was also virtually no water pressure which meant showering was not so much a refreshing pleasure but a slow chore. We rang Jersey Water to see about changing to mains water and were told that the nearest mains water pipe ran through the field across the road from our house.

'We'll have to check with the farmer who owns it,' advised the man we spoke to. He did indeed check and said the farmer was happy for us to have the water when they harvested the potato crop. Great, we thought, in just over a month or so we can get the water connected.

Meanwhile Oscar was happy indoors. For the first time in his short life he took an interest in the television. He was very selective in his viewing: he liked two programmes and one commercial, everything else he could leave. Luckily for him, one of his favourites, *Springwatch*, was on every evening. The programme followed the fauna of the British countryside as new life emerged across the land. Hidden cameras focused on birds in the nest ranging from little ringed plovers, goldcrests and reed buntings, to the familiar garden bird-table visitors such as great tits, greenfinches, robins and sparrows. The little squawking nestlings provided great entertainment for Oscar; he pawed the television trying to catch them as they hopped across the screen at ten times their actual size. The combination of movement and sound was irresistible to a cat, that at that moment was unable to climb trees and get the real thing. He was also particularly fond of the otters that featured on a programme called *Animal Park*, about the safari park at Longleat, one of England's finest stately homes. The programme followed the daily routine of the park and featured an array of animals from gorillas and tigers to giraffes and lions as well as many smaller species. Oscar had no interest in most of the menagerie, but as soon as he saw the otters darting in and out of the water, he was transfixed, totally mesmerised by animals he would be unlikely to ever see in real life.

'He's too close to the telly, he'll ruin his eyesight,' I said, not really sure if what I was saying was true. But he did like sitting literally within paw striking distance of the television when his favourites were on.

When he was not glued to his programmes, he liked to curl up on the sofa alongside Poppy who had by now forgiven him for being so stinky and seemed to enjoy his company once more. However, she was not so impressed if they were both sleeping and Oscar suddenly jumped up with a start and raced to the television.

'Oh no,' she must have thought, 'it's that advert again.'

Robinsons soft drinks were airing a brilliant advertisement featuring little birds that flew into what seemed from the outside, an ordinary nesting box, but inside it was revealed to be a state of the art 'human' apartment complete with furniture and fitted kitchen. The fridge, as well as containing the cordial that was being advertised, also had a packet of earthworms ready for the birds' tea. A human popped out of the cuckoo clock as it struck the hour. The crux of the advert was that the drink was made from naturally-sourced ingredients. You only noticed the detail on repeated viewings. For example as the birds entered the 'apartment' there were wellington boots in the shape of the birds' claws, on the television was a pigeon newscaster who had a picture of cat on the wall behind him in the guise of a wanted criminal. Obviously the humour was completely lost on Oscar but the hopping birds and their chirruping caused him no end of merriment. The advert is now on YouTube and if he could, Oscar would definitely have 'liked' it. Mike and I had as much amusement watching him being entertained as Oscar himself was having with his televisual habits.

Each day when we got home from work, the first thing we would do was go into the lounge and check on Oscar. Invariably he was waking up from a sleep, having a big stretch, and would meow as he came to greet us. He was not like a puppy though, bounding over; he would have to do the full sun salutation before he was ready. On this particular day I walked in the room to see the carpet absolutely covered with the unmistakable dried leaves of catnip. It did not take long to find further evidence of its provenance. Next to the computer was a box of dried catnip, which I had foolishly left on the dresser. Oscar must have scaled the chair by the computer, then hopped onto the dresser and knocked the box to the floor. He had chewed through both the box and the inner polythene bag to get his fix. He was even more mellow than usual that evening.

Getting stronger every day, Oscar seemed to be enjoying life more and more. His fur was growing back to its glossy black, although he was now sporting a white flash on his side flank from where the skin graft had been taken, and his tail also had a racoon-like ring of white fur where it had been run over in the accident.

He and Poppy explored the garden and he took great delight in following her up on to the shed roof to rustle the nesting blue tits. His paw–eye co-ordination was never a patch on Poppy's and he rarely appeared home triumphant with prey. One night however, he excelled himself. Oscar had a quiet meow, but sometimes he meowed in such a way that he almost sounded like a baby (if he was particularly in need of food). In fact, researchers at the University of Sussex discovered that cats use a 'soliciting purr' to gain attention from their owners. The study, led by Dr Karen McComb, found that the frequency of this purr was similar to a human baby's cry, thus provoking a response in the cat owner to react in some way, usually by feeding the cat. When he came through the cat flap and meowed, we knew we had to attend to him without delay. He trotted in to the kitchen and put down a plump field mouse next to his water bowl. Thankfully the mouse was already dead, so I did not have to worry about it scampering around the house. My mouse phobia is quite extreme and certainly at odds with living in the country with cats.

A couple of years earlier, when I was living in my flat and Lou was just past her prime but still had a bit of killer instinct in her, she'd brought in a mouse for me just before bedtime and dropped in on the carpet. I say she brought it in for me, but I think she'd actually brought it in solely for her own entertainment because the mouse was well and truly alive and seemed to be sporting no obvious injuries. Lou dropped it on the hall carpet and it immediately ran under one of the radiator covers.

'Oh my God, oh my God!' I shouted out loud as I witnessed what was going on. I immediately shut all the doors so the mouse was contained in the hallway and removed the radiator cover to try to get the mouse out.

'Kill it Lou!' I'd yelled at Lou, who had been watching it closely but not looking very likely to pounce. She'd started to purr loudly as she cornered the mouse without touching it.

Buzz was scratching on the other side of the lounge door keen to get in on the action. 'Maybe Buzz will kill it,' I thought in a blind panic. 'Perhaps I should let her out so she could help?' It suddenly occurred to me, rather contrarily, that the only way this mouse would live was by my intervention, but I was terrified of the poor little creature. I wanted Lou to kill the mouse, but at the same time I desperately did not want it to die. I remember looking at the defenceless creature in the corner with its little round eyes peeping out, knowing there was no way I could let it continue to be her plaything, so I threw Lou into the kitchen.

I stood in the hall with a mouse I was scared of, Buzz still scratching the lounge door and Lou meowing wildly from behind the kitchen door. I was frozen with terror and did not have a clue what to do. I thought about ringing the Animal Shelter, our local free facility for looking after pets and wildlife, but I was rational enough to know that it would be the emergency call-out service at that time of night, and they might be dealing with an incident of greater magnitude (although it was difficult to think what that might be). I decided I would ring my friend Ben who was very experienced at looking after cats but, unfortunately for me, he had gone to Switzerland to join his family for a week. I knew he would understand the stress I was going through, as he had been my flatmate until he left to move in with his partner. He also knew Buzz and Lou well.

I rushed into the kitchen to get my mobile phone and grabbed Lou at the same time before she could return to her mouse and pushed her back to the far end of the kitchen. I got the distinct feeling she would never have forgiven me, but at that moment, I had more important issues to deal with.

'Hi Ben, it's me,' I said in a panicked tone.

'Is everything OK? What's the matter?' he asked, sensing my concern.

'Lou's brought in a live mouse and I don't know what to do!'

Ben had burst out laughing. It was not the reaction I had hoped for at all.

'I'd come round and sort it out but it might take a couple of hours!' he'd continued, still giggling to himself.

'What shall I do?' I implored, as the little mouse continued to cower in the corner.

'Just pick it up at the base of its tail and throw it outside,' he'd advised, composing himself.

'What if it bites me?'

'It probably won't. Anyway, it'll be more scared of you, than you are of it.'

Why do people always say that? The mouse had no idea how scared I was.

'Kate,' Ben had said, who although twenty years my junior was, on this occasion, showing a sense of maturity that was clearly eluding me, 'just put some gloves on and throw it out. Ring me back when it's done.'

I just could not do it. I was a pathetic, lily-livered person, totally unable to deal with one of the basic occupational hazards of being a cat owner. I opened the front door and stood outside whilst I contemplated who I could call to come round and assist me. It was almost eleven o'clock on a Sunday evening, so I had to choose carefully.

To my absolute amazement the mouse trotted

down the hallway, over the base frame of the front doorstep and outside. Stunned, I ran inside quickly shutting the door behind me. Had that really happened? I opened the front door again and saw the mouse darting off into the flower beds, no doubt highly traumatised by having been caught by a giant grey cat, and then screamed at by a madwoman.

I then rang Ben and told him what had happened.

'That's hilarious. It probably would have jumped through the cat flap if you had left him to it!' he'd laughed. I do not know if my histrionics had resonated with Buzz and Lou, but that was the last occasion either of them ever brought in live prey.

Oscar, as I've mentioned already, was not the most proficient hunter in the household, that accolade belonged to Poppy. However, on this day it was Oscar who was bringing home his wares.

Having dropped the mouse by the side of his water bowl, he proceeded to eat his chicken dinner. Clearly this mouse was solely for entertainment and not nutrition. Once he'd finished eating, he picked up the mouse in his mouth and stood there, seemingly unsure of what to do next. Mike was standing next to him.

'Well done boy, you're very clever!' he praised him. Oscar meowed a response, and in doing so, dropped the mouse into the water bowl. Not so clever after all.

Mike and I burst out laughing. We should have known how humiliated Oscar would be as he flicked his tail up in a proverbial 'V' sign and departed for the front door, leaving his prey and his two annoying parents in the kitchen to clean up.

'Never thought he had it in him,' laughed Mike as he scooped the mouse from the water and dropped it in the bin.

'Can you take the bin out, just in case it's not properly dead?' I said, coming back to reality.

'Kate, it's not in a coma. It was bitten in the neck, had its spinal cord broken and was then drowned. It is an ex-mouse,' replied Mike and I had to put my trust in him. Later, when I was in bed, I was sure I heard scratching and scuffling on the landing.

CHAPTER 6

HERE WE GO AGAIN

By April of 2009, life had returned to normal. Oscar was fully recovered (apart from a small piece of skin underneath his leg which still had no fur growth on it), and was living life to the full. By now he was about 2 inches longer than Poppy, who still looked like a big kitten. Buzz was still ignoring Lou, apart from the occasional hiss as she walked past. She was, however, fascinated with Poppy, rushing to sniff her when she came in from one of her adventures. Poppy took it all in her stride. She knew she was alpha-cat-in-waiting and one day her turn would come. Becoming a teenager in cat years brought about a change in Poppy. She decided to move out.

By the side of our house are some old barns, which look ripe for conversion into a beautifully located des res, but in the meantime they have been unoccupied for many years, apart from playing temporary home to visiting house martins each summer. Poppy found it to be an ideal den and the old garden-seat mattresses that were piled on the ground made a comfortable bed. The door was wedged ajar and the window had no glass in it, allowing constant access. It was largely wind and waterproof and there was a ready supply of mice. Furthermore, there were no people or cats to pester her. She did not want to play with her pesky brother; Lou was so dull she was of no interest, and yes, she would go and see Buzz now and again; but people she could do without. The house became a place she visited only for meals and she would not hang around and socialise. There were things to do, places to see, mice to catch. Sometimes she did not return for over twenty-four hours, and conscious of what had happened to Oscar we would look for her and call her. When Poppy did come for food, Oscar was there like a shot, whether it was admiration for her independence or whether he wanted to get her to try to be friends with him we did not know, but she, for her part, was not in the slightest bit interested in him.

Poppy also knew exactly when she was meant to be close to home for her visit to the vet's for her vaccination. We made the appointment for as late as possible at 6.30 p.m. thinking that would give us a good hour after we got back from work to get her home. She would usually come in for a snack at around 5.30 p.m., but needless to say on this particular day she was nowhere to be seen. We called and called. We walked down the lane calling. We tapped the food bowls. Nothing. We knew she never came on demand, but this was a time-pressing matter. We also knew that she now lived life strictly on her terms, but she had an appointment to keep. She must have known that the vet's beckoned. Eventually, at about 6.20 p.m. we gave up our search and rang to cancel her appointment. They told us it happened all the time. She finally came home at about 7.30 p.m., seemingly knowing the practice would by now be closed.

Oscar was the complete opposite; he would jump on the bed in the morning to alert you to the fact that it was feeding time. In the evening he was in and out of the cat flap like a jack in the box, just in case there was more food in the offing. We seriously considered changing it for a revolving door. He curled up on our laps and loved a cuddle. When you called his name he came charging back, although this was probably because he knew he was generally only called when it was meal time and he liked to be at the front of the queue. Whether it was because he had met so many people when he was at the vet's or whether it was just in his nature, he was very good with humans. He liked being stroked by Mike's children or other visitors and all in all was your perfect pet cat.

When his routine altered, we took it very seriously. It was late April, about 10:30 at night and Oscar had not been in for dinner. That in itself caused alarm bells to ring.

'I'm going to look for him,' said Mike.

'He'll be back soon,' I replied, 'now it's getting warmer in the evenings he's bound to stay out later.'

Although generally I was the worrier in the family, Mike surpassed me when it came to the cats. I was now so used to Poppy hardly ever appearing, I thought Oscar too was gaining in confidence and exploring the fields around us at night.

Mike called and called but there was no sight or sound of him. He came back to fetch the torch.

'I'm just going up the road to see if I can see him,' he said grimly.

'Where are you Oscar?' I shouted out loud.

Less than five minutes later Mike returned.

'I've found this in the main road.'

'No!' I shrieked. It was Oscar's collar, snapped in two.

Hurriedly I put on my shoes and grabbed another torch.

'I can't see him by the road,' Mike said as we walked to the front of the house. Traffic was light at this time of night, but the occasional car illuminated the road, but there were no signs of Oscar and encouragingly, no sign of blood either.

'I'm going into the field,' I told Mike, clambering through the brambles and yew that made up the hedge, entering at the point in the road where he had found the collar.

'Oscar! Oscar!' we both called.

'He can't be far away,' reasoned Mike, but there was no sign. Being black it was hard to see Oscar in the dark. Occasional rustles caught our attention, but on closer inspection it was merely the wind in the plants. Mike, having taken the torch to search down both sides of the main road, had also switched his attention to the field, which was planted with sprouting Jersey Royal potatoes.

'Remember last time? He got himself home, so he might be trying to do the same,' reasoned Mike.

'I'll go and have a look to see if he's nearer the house then,' I replied.

I left that part of the field and headed along the

road towards the house. I heard a little cry.

'Oscar,' I said in soothing tones. I heard it again. It was coming from the field directly opposite our house. I shone my torch and there he was, curled in a ball at the entrance to a culvert that ran from the field, under the road, to our house. Fortunately the dry weather of late meant it had no water in it.

'I've found him!' I yelled to Mike who was still in the field.

'He's down in the culvert. Can you grab him?' I was the wrong side of the hedge so it was easier for Mike to scoop him up as he quickly made his way through the potato crop.

Mike got down and gently picked him up.

'He's freezing,' exclaimed Mike as Oscar whimpered in his arms.

We brought him back into the house and put him down carefully on the lounge floor. There was no obvious sign of damage but when he tried to stand up he collapsed onto the floor. I rang New Era Veterinary Hospital and said we needed to see a vet and once again we put him into the cat carrier (now with a new collection of cobwebs on it) and took him over there.

'We were hoping we wouldn't see you again!' said Kerry, the nurse, to Oscar as she unlocked the doors to let us through.

The duty vet examined Oscar and confirmed what we thought: that he had been hit by a car. He said he was in shock and they would keep him in overnight and thoroughly examine him. The vet took him through to the back of the practice where the nurses would administer pain relief and when he came back I asked,

'Don't cats learn their lesson after they've been

hit by a car once?'

'Not always, some of them just don't have much road sense—or are unlucky.' Oscar was probably both, I thought.

'Is Oscar insured?' he continued as he filled out the 'paperwork' on the computer.

'Yes, he is,' Mike answered. That was a mistake we were determined not to make twice. As soon as Oscar had had his previous accident (the bill for which we were still paying), we had taken out pet insurance. I had never had it for Buzz or Lou, but for a fairly modest premium we thought it would be worthwhile.

We headed back to the cottage leaving Oscar to spend yet another night in his second home.

The next morning Peter, who was back on duty, rang us.

'He's dislocated his hip,' he explained, 'but in true Oscar style it's not straightforward; he's abnormally dislocated it.' Here we go again, I thought, as Peter continued, 'Usually with a dislocation you can put the ball back into the socket with some manipulation, but as Oscar seems to have somehow twisted it awkwardly, we're going to have to cut him open and put a toggle in.'

Oscar was not yet two years old and including his neutering, this would be his fourth major operation.

'OK,' replied Mike, 'we'll wait to hear from you and hopefully pop down to see him later.'

The operation was a success and we were allowed to visit him in the all-too-familiar surroundings of the post-operative kennels. He had been shaved again all over his left-hind side and the row of stitches was covered with a dressing. He was wearing an Elizabethan collar again and generally

71

looking rather sad. We opened the door to his kennel and stroked him. He let out a gentle purr, but was clearly still tired from the anaesthetic and the trauma of his accident.

Peter came through and explained that we could take Oscar home in a day or two and that he was pleased with how the operation had gone. We once again felt very lucky to have Peter as our vet. Not only had he twice put Oscar back together again, but it was also Peter who had insisted that we put a collar on Oscar. Had Mike not found the collar in the road, we would almost certainly not have been so persistent in our search for him. We may well have waited until morning, by which time it would have been very likely that Oscar would have died of shock.

'Oscar, you're getting through your nine lives too quickly. Can you slow down a bit?' I said to him as I gently stroked him.

A few days later, Oscar came home. He had a slight limp and once again the indignity of having no fur on his left side.

It was so sad to see him weighed down by the collar. His head was held low as he padded about the lounge where he was incarcerated until further notice. Again we went through the routine of getting his medicine down him as we had earlier in the year. He knew he had to have it and we put it on his food and he wolfed it down as he always had done. We were grateful it was not in tablet form.

As any cat owner will tell you, one of the most challenging times between a cat and its owner is when it comes to the administering of pills. What is also astonishing is how vets and veterinary nurses can pop a pill down a cat's throat with the greatest of ease. Practice makes perfect, I guess. I came across this description of giving a tablet to a cat on www.rulingcatsanddogs.com. I have modified it slightly, but the gist is the same:

1. Pick up cat and cradle in the crook of your left arm as if holding a baby. Position right forefinger and thumb on either side of cat's mouth and gently apply pressure to cheek while holding pill in right hand. As cat opens mouth, pop pill into mouth. Allow cat to close mouth and swallow.

2. Retrieve pill from floor and cat from behind sofa and repeat process.

3. Retrieve cat from sofa and throw away soggy pill.

4. Take new pill from foil wrapper, cradle cat in left arm, holding rear paws tightly with left hand. Force jaws open and push pill to back of mouth with right forefinger. Hold mouth shut for a count of ten.

5. Retrieve pill from goldfish bowl and cat from top of wardrobe. Pull spouse from garden.

6. Kneel on floor with cat wedged firmly between knees, holding front and rear paws. Ignore low growl emitted by cat. Get spouse to hold cat's head firmly with one hand while forcing wooden ruler into mouth. Drop pill down ruler and rub cat's throat vigorously.

7. Retrieve cat from curtain rail, get another pill from foil wrapper. Make note to buy new ruler and repair curtains. Carefully sweep shattered figurines from hearth and set to one side for gluing later.

8. Wrap cat in large towel and get spouse to lie on cat with its head just visible from below spouse's armpit. Put pill in end of drinking straw; force cat's mouth open with pencil and blow down drinking straw.

9. Check label to make sure pill not harmful to humans, drink glass of water to take taste away. Apply bandage to spouse's forearm and remove blood from carpet with cold water and soap.

10. Retrieve cat from neighbour's shed. Get another pill. Place cat in cupboard and close door onto neck to leave head showing. Force mouth open with dessertspoon. Flick pill down throat with elastic band.

11. Fetch screwdriver from garage and put door back on hinges. Apply cold compress to cheek and check records for date of last tetanus shot. Throw T-shirt away and fetch new one from bedroom.

12. Ring fire brigade to retrieve cat from tree across the road. Apologise to neighbour who crashed into fence whilst swerving to avoid cat. Take last pill from foil wrapper.

13. Tie cat's front paws to rear paws with garden twine and bind tightly to leg of dining table. Find heavy-duty pruning gloves from shed. Force cat's mouth open with small spanner. Push pill into mouth followed by large piece of fillet steak. Hold head vertically and pour pint of water down throat to wash pill down.

14. Get spouse to drive you to hospital; sit quietly while doctor stitches finger and forearm and removes pill remnants from right eye. Stop by furniture shop on way home to order new table.

Of course, this is greatly exaggerated and clearly never came down to using screwdrivers and the like, but as any cat owner will tell you, the administration of pills is tricky to say the least.

In fact, what we usually did with Poppy was crush the tablets and put them in a nice piece of fresh fish. I'm not sure how she managed to do it, but somehow she invariably managed to lick around the fine powder of the tablets, leaving not a morsel of fish but a bowl lined with the pink residue of rejected medication. Oscar, on the other hand, was not particularly happy to have pills put in his mouth (it was extraordinary just how long he could keep his mouth closed without swallowing it), but he would lick his plate clean if it involved fish. A crushed-up tablet was not going to put him off his meal.

We kept him in throughout May and although the weather was warming up he seemed settled in the lounge and did not hanker to go out with the other three cats. To keep him entertained we bought him a regular supply of knitted hedgehogs or 'hoggies', as they were christened in our household. These were handmade in Jersey, knitted in a variety of colours and filled with what seemed to be Class A catnip, as the cats went wild for them. We could buy factory-made mice filled with catnip or dried catnip on its own (to be liberally sprinkled round the scratching post) or super-strength catnip chews, but nothing had the impact of these 'hoggies', sold for 75p each in aid of saving injured hedgehogs in Jersey.

They held no end of entertainment for our cats. According to them, the correct way to attack a hoggy (for they must be destroyed), is to firstly rub your cheeks on it to release the oils, then grab it between your front paws, roll onto your side or back and use your back paws to scratch it apart. Repeat regularly for several days until a hole appears in the wool. Grab the hoggy in your front paw, and then use your mouth to tug open the hoggy. Continue until the catnip is released on the carpet. Roll over. Lose interest. New hoggy appears. Repeat process.

In the unlikely event of anyone asking if Oscar has done anything for charity, we can safely say that he has been instrumental in preserving the hedgehog population of Jersey.

After about three weeks, we got the clearance from Peter to allow Oscar out and decided to adopt a different approach. Rather than letting him roam freely, we invested in a cat harness so we could take him for walks. This would allow him to enjoy the smell of the countryside and get some exercise, but we would have full control over where he was, thus keeping him out of danger. He was such a yielding cat and responded so well to human intervention, we thought he would be an ideal candidate for adapting to being restrained in this manner.

The pet shop stocked an array of styles and colours, pink with diamanté—maybe not, he was probably having bad enough issues with his self-esteem as it was. Black was a safe option, but rather dull; the camouflage ones were a bit different, but the fact that he was black and had been camouflaged in the dark of the night when his accident happened led us to buy a luminous green one. This one would ensure that, in the unlikely event of him being out at night with it, he would be seen in headlights. But more to the point, the colour would look really good against his black fur.

We followed the instructions:

Ensure you have a comfortably fitting harness and lightweight lead with a secure clip. Do not use a collar, as the cat may be able to slip out of it. You want the lead to pull from the chest rather than the throat.

Done, purchased and ready to attach.

Put the harness and lead somewhere near sleeping area and leave it there for several days to accustom him to its appearance and smell.

Well, we wafted it in front of his nose, but he thought it was part of his physiotherapy routine and leapt for it like one of his long-forgotten mice.

Wait until just before his normal mealtime, then

put the harness on the cat. You should be able to comfortably slip two fingers between the harness and his skin.

We decided to wait until after his mealtime, thinking he would be more compliant if he had eaten.

Immediately feed him his favourite meal and praise him when he is finished.

Right, we had done this the wrong way round. Oscar was starting to get a bit wriggly.

Let him wear the harness for a while.

If it seems to bother him, distract him by playing with a favourite toy.

He was now shaking with the same degree of alacrity as many a human would do if a spider fell down their top.

When your cat seems to be accustomed to the harness, take it off.

We did not have to complete step six as Oscar had managed to rid himself of it.

We repeated the process the next day, this time following the instructions in the right order. It was no good; as soon as Oscar had the harness on he leapt around the place shaking his head and body like a Labrador coming out of the sea. He did not like it one bit. I worried he was going to damage his hip with so much leaping about. He bared his teeth, he growled, it was an Oscar we did not know. We left the harness casually lying around so he would get used to it, but every time Mike or I went to move it, Oscar would growl and run away.

'It's for your own good Oscar,' I would tell him. 'You know you want to go outside.'

'Not with that thing on I don't,' I sensed he was telling me.

If I had carried on and followed the rest of the instructions (there were fifteen in total), I would have read that perseverance was the key and you were meant to repeat daily until the cat accepted it. I was thinking more along the lines that if you can't teach an old dog new tricks you have even less hope with a young cat. We gave up. We were going to have to let him roam freely or not at all. We opted for the former.

Soon Oscar was going out and about in the day. His hip was repairing well and he was jumping and climbing as well as he could before. The limp had gone and he nimbly negotiated the walls and fences that surround our house. We kept him in at night whilst we tried to indoctrinate him with the Green Cross Code. We were worried about him being outside at night, but stood by our beliefs that he should have the right to roam. As far as we were aware (i.e. probably not very) Oscar never went far. We could often see him from our bedroom window wandering in the field opposite, stalking potential prey. We startled him completely once when we went for a walk and stumbled upon him about three fields away from our house.

'What the . . .' he seemed to be saying, 'what are YOU doing here?'

Nonetheless, he would come if he was called and

was never late for a meal.

'Perhaps he has finally learned his lesson,' I said to Mike portentously.

CHAPTER 7

SUN AND SPUDS

As the weather continued to improve and spring bloomed into summer, the cats were spending more and more time outside. The ancient wisteria that grew around our front door and bedroom windows was a mass of lilac fronds. The honeysuckle that grew wild over the barn was in full bloom, emitting its strong, evocative scent each evening as dusk fell. Poppy had moved out of the barn and now resided in a nest of leaves at the back of the garden. She was an outdoor cat in the true sense of the word.

The Jersey Royal potatoes in the field opposite our house were ready for harvesting. The kidney-shaped potatoes have been grown in Jersey since the mid-eighteenth century. By 1810, the once famous cider orchards had vanished from Jersey and growers were experimenting with exporting new potatoes to England for the early summer trade due to their popularity. The Jersey Royal was first known as the Jersey Royal Fluke due to the circumstances by which it originated. The story goes that around 1880 a farmer, called Hugh de la Haye, hosted a dinner party at which he showed his friends two large potatoes that he had bought in a local store. One had fifteen 'eyes' (from which new plants sprout) and so they decided to cut the potatoes up, plant them and wait to see what would happen. The following spring a crop appeared and whilst most were the normal round shape, one crop produced kidney-shaped potatoes, which he called the Jersey Royal Fluke. The potatoes soon became known as Jersey Royals, a name by which they have been called ever since.

Today, the Jersey Royal is still the very first new potato of the season remaining unique in taste and quality thanks to the sun-soaked *côtils* (steep south-facing slopes that benefit from the maximum amount of sunshine) and the rich soil in which they are grown. Such is its popularity, that in 2012, world-famous London department store Selfridges set up a waiting list which allowed customers to register interest in the early crop. It is the only vegetable to have the Protected Designation of Origin status (meaning they can only be grown in Jersey) and if they are grown elsewhere they are simply 'new potatoes'. For his part in developing them, Hugh de la Haye was honoured by the islanders at a formal gathering with a testimonial and a purse of gold sovereigns.

Whether the potatoes in the field opposite us would end up in a UK supermarket or in our local shops was unclear, but with their harvest came a sign that summer was well and truly on the way.

We were delighted that the harvest was taking place as it meant that, once complete, work could start on digging in the field to secure mains water for our house. We rang Jersey Water as soon as we saw the potato pickers in the field.

'I'm afraid it's not good news,' said Mick, our man at Jersey Water. 'The farmer is going to plant a crop of maize more or less immediately and he won't let us work in the field until that is harvested.'

'When will that be?' I asked, indignant that I wasn't able to get the water immediately.

'Probably mid-September,' replied Mick. That was months away. So much for a summer of being blonde. It was very disappointing news. Indeed, over the following week the field was ploughed and seeds were planted in the place of the potatoes, which would bring forth a sea of maize in the coming months.

Water or no water, we continued to have work done on the house and June saw us having the gable end rendered. As the two workmen, Callum and Ronan, hacked off the unsightly, cracked plaster, Oscar found the most amazing litter tray. We had had a skip delivered full of sand for the new render, and Oscar took no time at all in making his mark there. He visited it several times a day despite our protestations. We can safely say that our new gable end has a little bit of him in it.

A few weeks after the rendering was finished we were really starting to enjoy the summer. It was the sort of day Jersey Tourism would use to feature in their brochures and on calendars. The sun, high in the midsummer sky, shone continuously. The light sea breeze barely caused the leaves on the trees to stir. The heavy rain which had fallen earlier in the week brought lushness to the surrounding fields. In the garden the intense greens of the foliage contrasted with the bright reds and pinks of the geraniums in full bloom. The lobelia spilled over their terracotta pots as they competed for space with pink petunias and ballerina-like fuchsias. Brambles were laden with green blackberries, which a month later I would forage for warming autumn puddings. In the distance the sea twinkled and glinted in the sun.

All four cats were outside, lazing around like a pride of lions in the Kalahari. Oscar and Poppy were too young and energetic to stay still for very long though and they soon disappeared on one of their adventures. I was on annual leave and spent most of the day reading in the garden—a rare pleasure.

After he had had a busy day at work, I poured Mike a cooling glass of lemonade whilst he unwound in the sun. I then deadheaded a few roses that had passed their peak, before unravelling the hosepipe to water the numerous pots and containers.

By mid evening, Buzz, Lou and Poppy were in the kitchen ready for food. The heat did not appear to diminish their appetites. Mike put their fish in the microwave as the girls impatiently circled the kitchen, letting out the 'I am going to die of starvation and ring Cats Protection if you don't feed me now' cry. But where was Oscar? He was usually first in the queue for food, especially on fish nights when he seemed to be able to smell it from a 50-yard radius and come running. Thinking about it I had not seen Oscar since about eleven o'clock that morning and it was now approaching eight in the evening. If Poppy had disappeared for this amount of time, we would not have been unduly worried, but Oscar had a history of getting himself into trouble.

'Let's go and look for him,' sighed Mike. Please don't make this third time unlucky, I thought to myself.

We wandered down the lanes calling for Oscar.

We looked in the culvert where we had found him last time; we walked down the busier road, poking under the hawthorns that edged the fields. We changed direction and walked down other lanes. A big, black cloud was overshadowing the beauty of the day. Oscar had not missed dinner since he was hit by a car in April. We called and we called. There was no reply.

We decided to bring in reinforcements and asked Tracey if she would join in the search. She came round and we agreed to go in different directions. We took a towel each in case we needed to wrap him up when we found him. We trespassed in fields, crossed over streams, poked about in disused agricultural greenhouses looking for him. A passer-by that Tracey asked said he thought he had seen him on the neighbouring football pitch, but a search there proved fruitless. As dusk fell we returned home, our spirits as damp as the dew that was forming on the grass. Not again, surely not.

We could not talk to each other; we were all in our own worlds, wondering what had happened to him now. I looked up on the Internet how many miles a cat could roam in case we should go back out and extend our search. Typically information varied from not very far at all to several miles. Oscar was microchipped and we half expected a call from the Animal Shelter to say he had been found in a bad way. We knew he was not the most road-savvy cat and even Peter, the vet, said some cats just do not learn from a bad experience and will go on to have further accidents.

'I had better go and get us some dinner,' Mike wearily said as we brought the search to a temporary close. It was almost dark by now.

He headed off to the local Chinese to grab a takeaway, but returned half an hour later empty-handed, having forgotten to take his wallet, what with all the distractions of the day. He grabbed it and headed back to pick up what would now be lukewarm chilli beef and Singapore noodles. Not being particularly hungry, we half ate the congealed mess, more for nourishment (of sorts) than for enjoyment. As we stood in the kitchen putting the foil trays in the bin and the plates in the dishwasher, Oscar appeared, tail in the air, meowing.

'Is he OK?' I asked, momentarily transported back to when he dragged himself home at Christmas.

'Seems to be,' replied Mike as Oscar wrapped himself round his legs and picked him up. Oscar purred loudly.

'He stinks of the field!' exclaimed Mike and so he did. There was a definite grass smell about him and his fur was totally dry as if all the oil had been removed. Other than that he seemed to have managed to return unscathed from his twelve-hour adventure. As we fussed and patted him, his only priority was to eat his long-overdue fish, which looked a lot more appetising than our Chinese had been. We have heard many tales of cats who have disappeared for considerably longer than this, however, with Oscar's history every hour felt like a day for us.

The schools broke up for the long summer holidays and tourists flocked to the island. 'Bucket and spade' tourism has gradually declined and the development of several stunning luxury hotels has now started to attract the top-end short-break market. As usual, the summer weather did not quite live up to our expectations, a few sunny days here and there with temperatures slightly above the national average. When we had the rendering done it was unbelievably hot, resulting in the plasterers having to return on a regular basis to hose the wall so it did not dry too quickly. We wanted to get as much done to the house as possible in the summer months, but we could not proceed with the major internal works of the kitchen and bathroom until we had mains water. Watching the maize grow so rapidly was very exciting for us as it meant that it would not be too long until the harvest and our water supply were connected.

Finally, harvest day came.

CHAPTER 8

THE BIG ONE

Summer was drawing to a close, but still the sun shone brightly on that fateful Friday morning. Mike was taking the day off to concentrate on decorating our bedroom. Weekends were busy with the usual chores of laundry, shopping and cleaning as well as collecting his son, Chris. Rachael, Mike's daughter, had just returned to university near Liverpool to start the second year of her degree. There didn't seem to be much time to do things like decorating without having to take annual leave. It was the start of a lucky sequence of events that would save Oscar's life that day.

I steered well clear of the work-in-progress that

was my home and went to work at my job as a recruitment manager in St Helier. It was a beautiful day, made even better in the morning when I received a phone call from Mike.

'They're harvesting the field,' he told me.

'Excellent, that's fantastic news!' I replied.

We were delighted they were finally harvesting the maize in the huge field directly opposite our home. We had been joking to each other about the time last year after harvest when we had sneaked into the field and picked up some discarded corncobs, boiled them up and served them with lashings of Jersey butter. They tasted vile; they were dry and definitely not sweet. It hadn't crossed our minds that the crop had been animal fodder and not for human consumption at all! That was the last time we helped ourselves to the farmer's leftovers.

'Get on the phone to Jersey Water,' I said to Mike excitedly. 'Quick, before they plant anything else!'

Mike called back more or less straightaway.

'I've spoken to them; they're going to speak to the farmer and schedule the work for the next couple of weeks. They haven't got any more crops going in immediately.'

Fabulous. We could even get a dishwasher now. Much as I loved living in a period cottage, the lack of creature comforts was starting to become a drag.

It was a good day for me at the office too. We were heading towards the end of the month with excellent results to report, in fact we were going to be almost 10 per cent above our target, which in difficult trading conditions was a great achievement by the team.

Our small office of ten people definitely had a

good 'Friday Feeling' that day. Great results, bacon sandwiches (a Friday treat) and a hot, late-summer weekend looming. We were all in a buoyant frame of mind and looking forward to four o'clock when the wine would be opened and we could round off the week with a tipple and a chat.

Then at 3.30 p.m. I received a phone call that I will never forget. Mike's mobile number came up on my telephone as my direct line started ringing. 'That's odd,' I thought, 'why isn't he calling from the landline if he's at home busy decorating? Perhaps he's nipped to the shops and wants to know what I fancy for dinner?'

'I'm at the vet's,' said Mike breathlessly. I knew instantly which cat it was. Of our four cats there was only one who was always in trouble. Only one known on sight to all the vets at the practice. Only one who had already had two serious accidents in the space of less than a year.

'It's Oscar,' said Mike, unnecessarily. 'There's been an accident in the field. I think his leg has been taken off.'

He went on. I tried to process what he was telling me.

'Oh my God! Oh my God!' I cried. 'What's happening to him now?'

'Peter's taken him through.'

Peter. Oscar's saviour twice before. Even without knowing exactly what had happened, I knew he couldn't be in better hands.

'Please can you collect me from work now,' my voice wobbling as I burst into tears. I was confused as to what had happened and started shaking so strongly that my boss opened the Friday afternoon wine early to help me calm down. I started seeing a flickering light above my head, almost how I'd imagine a migraine to be. I'd never had a migraine but sensed I might be having my first one. What had Oscar done now?

Mike collected me and told me what had happened. He was upstairs, stripping the woodchip paper from the bedroom walls whilst watching the combine harvester and the tractor driving up and down the field opposite. The maize had been fascinating to watch over the past few months because it had grown so incredibly fast. Now, however, we were pleased to see that it was going.

At mid afternoon there was a knock on the door. We don't get many callers, as apart from our neighbours on either side, we're on our own and relatively isolated. Apart from people we knew were dropping by, it was only the occasional visit from the Jehovah's Witnesses or delivery drivers with our Internet shopping who turned up at unpredictable times. Mike answered to find a distressed-looking woman standing with a bicycle.

'Have you got a black cat?' she asked, probably not knowing if it was better if Mike said 'yes' or 'no'.

'Yes, I have.'

'I think it's in trouble, there's a black cat in the field and there's a lot of blood. I think it might have been hit by a car!' she exclaimed.

Mike thanked her and rushed out of the house into the lane. Tracey was also at our house, having popped round to borrow one of my books, and was sitting in the garden waiting for me to get back from work. The noise of the combine harvester and tractor was still very loud although harvesting was almost done. Mike shouted to Tracey, who had heard the doorbell but was oblivious to the commotion.

'Grab a towel and come with me. It's Oscar!' yelled Mike to Tracey who swiftly scooped up the towel from the lounger and joined Mike to race down the road.

'He's just in there,' pointed out the passer-by who had led the way, leaving her bicycle lying on the drive. The side of the road and the hedgerow that bordered the field were spattered with blood and sure enough, there was Oscar lying at the edge of the field. It looked as if he had been trying to drag himself home but couldn't quite manage it, so had retreated to the field. Tracey picked him up and passed him to Mike. A claw seemed to be stuck in his belly and his leg appeared to be missing. Tracey (who had been a qualified nurse) wrapped him tightly in the towel to try and stem any bleeding; he was dripping blood from his back end. Neither Mike nor Tracey looked too closely.

Mike rang New Era Veterinary Hospital (we had them on speed dial) and explained what had happened. Running back towards the house, Mike got in the car whilst Tracey sat with Oscar on the back seat. This was no time to go ferreting around to find the cat carrier. It was only about a mile's drive to the practice, but it seemed to take them forever. At a busy junction, Mike eventually found a gap in the traffic and pulled out only to be held up further on by the school crossing. Finally they arrived and Oscar meowed quietly in the back of the car. Mike hadn't even put on his seat belt. He was a cat ambulance. He raced into the building, barging through the double doors into reception.

Amanda, one of the fantastic nurses, was waiting

for them.

'Oh God, it's YOUR Oscar! When they said be prepared for Oscar, I thought it couldn't be him again!' she exclaimed.

'Yeah, I'm afraid it is,' Mike couldn't quite believe it either.

The crash team was ready for him. Peter Haworth, the vet who knew Oscar only too well, came out and took Oscar from Mike. All the colour drained from Mike's face as he explained what had happened.

'They're harvesting the field opposite us. I think Oscar must have been caught by the combine harvester. I'm not really sure how it happened.'

'Look,' replied Peter, almost with as much disbelief as Mike, 'I'm going to take a look at him, and make him comfortable. I'll call you later.'

Mike was in total shock. Not just because he had never seen anything quite so gruesome, it was more that poor Oscar had been unbelievably brave in the past year, and now this had happened.

Soppy Oscar, the friendly headbutting cat. The most sweet-natured, cuddliest cat we had ever known. Oscar who was loved by everyone who met him. He wasn't skittish and nervous like his sister Poppy. He wasn't cantankerous like his older stepsister Buzz or aloof like Buzz's sister Lou. He was gentle, affectionate and loving. He never scratched or bit, even when in extreme pain. After everything he had been through we had been so happy that he had had a brilliant summer playing in the fields. For it to all end like this seemed too horrific to bear.

We sat at home that night, numb to the core. It seemed so much worse because it was Oscar. Not that we didn't love our other three cats, they all brought us a great deal of pleasure—'our girls' as we collectively called them—but Oscar was special. He had been a survivor, but now there didn't seem to be any hope. He had recovered from his other operations because he had received amazing medical care, he was young and the injuries were recoverable.

But how could he possibly get through this? Peter had called to say both his back feet had been amputated around the ankle. BOTH his feet! We were stunned. We knew it was bad but we didn't realise it was this bad.

We couldn't imagine what would happen next. As we sat there on that miserable Friday evening, we reflected on Oscar's life. It had been a life punctuated by trips to the vet, but for the last three months he had been fit and happy.

We reminisced about how we had watched him trying to catch a mouse under the rose bush only a week before. We were standing at the kitchen window as he sniffed out the little rodent. He pawed it and it got away. He persisted and got it under his paws again, faltered, and the mouse made its exit. Oscar persevered and eventually got it in his mouth. Then he seemed a bit unsure about what to do next. He dropped it and grabbed it in his paws again. After about fifteen minutes of literally playing cat and mouse, Oscar finally had his quarry, or so he thought. He was momentarily distracted by the sound of an overhead plane and the mouse took its chances and fled. Defeated, Oscar sat down under the rose bush, probably wondering where it had all gone wrong. To add to his humiliation, Buzz, a cat who was well past her prime, ventured under the rose bush herself a short while later and triumphantly caught said mouse.

'Well there'll be no more mice for Oscar,' I said.

'Don't be like that,' replied Mike, 'he might be all right.'

'Don't be ridiculous, how can a cat live on two paws?' I asked.

'Well dogs can. They have those wheel things.'

'Yeah but dogs are completely different from cats. I think we have got to think about what's best for Oscar. If we have to let him go, we'll have to remember what a lovely summer he's had.'

'Kate, will you stop talking like that!' Mike exclaimed.

'I don't want Oscar to go any more than you, but we've got to be realistic,' I said.

And so the conversation went on, talking round and round in circles, neither of us really wanting to face up to the truth; that as far as we knew, there was really no hope for Oscar, and that tomorrow we would have to say goodbye. We tried to imagine what had actually happened that afternoon. We couldn't understand how he had not been able to get away from the combine harvester. We also couldn't really understand why it was pretty much just a clean cut across his back paws whilst the rest of him came out completely unscathed. We wondered if the farmer had been aware of what had happened. There were so many questions, but the one which weighed most heavily was what on earth was going to happen next?

'I've just thought,' Mike broke the silence, 'we never asked the lady what her name was.' We were sure the kind passer-by (who was on the way to pick her daughter up from school, Mike had told me later) would want to know what had happened to the cat and we had no way of finding out who she was.

Our thoughts returning to Oscar, we realised that we would have to gear ourselves up to have him put to sleep, although sleep was the one thing we couldn't do ourselves.

Luckily for Oscar, not everyone was as pessimistic as I was.

CHAPTER 9

THE REFERRAL

The weekend passed in a haze. The horrifying circumstances of the accident kept going through our mind. We spoke to Peter at the vet's to see if he had an idea as to what could have happened. His guess was that Oscar had been asleep in the cornfield and had become disoriented by the noise of the harvester, bearing in mind that the blades would be some way away from the noise of the engine. It is likely that Oscar rolled over and in doing so, had his paws severed. It is thought he then tried to drag himself home only he ran out of steam and went back to the field. The blood in the lane remained for weeks, a constant reminder of the gruesomeness of the event. Without doubt, if the passer-by had not knocked on the door and Mike had not been at home, Oscar would have died shortly afterwards, either of loss of blood or shock.

We went to visit Oscar at New Era. He was on a drip, but looked comfortable in his kennel. His legs were covered in yellow bandages with smiley faces on them. The vet had fashioned the bandages into the shape of little bootees, meeting the length of his two front paws. He looked up, his big round eyes full of sadness and we opened his cage and stroked the poor little chap.

'Oh Oscar, what have you done?' I asked, as he head-butted my hand.

His kennel was in a bank of twelve, four cages across and three high. Oscar was in one of the middle cages at eye level. We looked around at the other cats. The cards on the front of their kennels gave their name and condition; Misty, in for spaying, Cleo, a cat with kidney trouble and Dizzy, a little ginger kitten that had been hit by car. All their owners would be worrying about their pets too. Selfishly, I thought, at least they can all recover. None of them have lost their feet.

Oscar was purring and nuzzling us as he normally did. From the waist up he looked in fine fettle. As the nurses came in and out of the kennel area to attend their patients, Kerry, a nurse we had come to know well, said, 'We couldn't believe it was Oscar AGAIN.'

'You wouldn't believe we've got three other cats at home!' retorted Mike. 'It's only Oscar who's ever here.

'I love seeing Oscar but not this often!' joked Kerry, who had developed an excellent bond with Oscar during his previous stays at New Era. Her affinity with the animals was wonderful. I think Oscar would have quite liked to have been adopted by her.

'And he's only two and a half!' I said, thinking that this must surely be his ninth if not tenth life.

It was a very strange time for us. It was hard to go about our daily business when we felt like we were in limbo. Oscar was comfortable and alive. He did not seem to be in pain, he wasn't crying or complaining. We were doing the crying for him. No one seemed to know what would happen next. No one would commit to saying it was time to let him go. The nurses at the New Era Veterinary Hospital were treating him as well as they always did. He was still eating, which frankly came as no surprise us. Whatever Oscar goes through, his appetite remains intact.

I wondered why we were keeping him alive. Mike and I had recently watched a TV programme about people who had pets with disabilities. These special needs animals had a range of conditions including a parrot that was on anti-depressants following the death of his owner, an incontinent cat who had to be 'evacuated' by being physically squeezed and a dog who rolled along on wheel castors. Despite admiring the bond between humans and their pets and the lengths people went to in order to give the animals a chance at life, my cynical self did wonder if it was always in the best interests of the animals. When the programme was shown again a few years later, my point of view had changed. I knew how it felt to want to do everything possible to preserve the life of your beloved pet as long as they were still able to have a fulfilling life.

We were resigned to Oscar's fate. Unless there was some miracle cure which could re-grow Oscar's feet, we felt this was it and that Oscar was being kept alive because no one really wanted to be the one to say that it was Game Over for Oscar. He had engendered such affection from the team at New

Era it was not a decision anyone would want to take lightly. He was our cat, so naturally we thought there was something a bit special about Oscar. It seemed, though, we were not alone and everyone wanted Oscar to live. The question was of course, what exactly could be done?

After a couple of days Peter had an idea. He explained to us that he knew of a vet in England (through a mutual friend in the USA) that had used implants for dogs to replace missing limbs. He said it was a total long shot but he was willing to talk to him if we were happy to do this. He said he didn't know if the vet would be interested, or indeed if it would be possible to do it at all. He couldn't say how much the treatment would cost. Peter was blunt, but honest with us. The choice was either to explore this option or euthanasia. We had thought as much. Suddenly we had a glimmer of hope at a time when we thought there was no hope left. We knew it was an extreme long shot, we knew it might not happen, we knew it might not work, we knew it might be prohibitively expensive. We also knew we had to explore this option fully. It was all we had.

Peter Haworth is an extraordinary vet. He treats animals with compassion and skill, he is clearly gifted and passionate about what he does, but at the same time he is totally down to earth and always has time to talk his patients' 'parents'. He had developed a bond with Oscar; although we are in no doubt that he treats all the animals equally, maybe Oscar was treated a little bit more equally than others. We knew that we were in the right place at the right time. A different vet, a different cat even, may have meant the end, but thankfully for Oscar, Peter knew of the incredible Noel

Fitzpatrick.

Peter contacted Noel who initially seemed interested. He acknowledged it was very unusual to get a bilateral amputation where the animal wasn't either instantly killed or put down by the vet. Furthermore, because Oscar was only two years old, his chances of survival were higher. Peter sent X-rays and pictures to Noel. Noel came back with queries. Over the course of the next few days, Noel built up a clear enough picture of Oscar's condition to agree in principle to go ahead with the surgery. He was keen to stress, though, that he could not commit to undertaking the surgery without examining Oscar thoroughly himself. The X-rays and emails from Peter were invaluable, however he needed to look at the site where the implants would go in order make an assessment of the actual viability of the operation. It was hard for us to not be excited and we had to stop ourselves from thinking that everything was going to be fine now we had located a potential saviour.

Oscar, meanwhile, was walking round on his padded stumps. Peter had stacked them up and put a splint on them to assist his walking. It was not pretty to watch. He moved awkwardly, kicking his back legs out as he moved forward. It was if they went into involuntary spasms. He was wobbly and uncoordinated but he was determined. He did not seem unduly fazed by his condition and he certainly did not seem depressed or anxious. He seemed to be coping fine. His eyes were bright and when we visited him daily, his eyes lit up further. In reality, it was probably our eyes that brightened, so pleased were we to see him. It was easy to forget, though, that under the bandages his feet were not growing back. The stumps were there and it was never going to be a case of a big reveal and new feet. That was hard to come to terms with.

Whilst Peter and Noel were discussing Oscar's future, Mike and I did our own soul searching.

'Wouldn't that be amazing if he got new feet?' said Mike.

'It would, but I'm just a bit scared. Are we doing the right thing? Don't you think Oscar has been through enough?' I asked. The truth was, we both felt guilty for potentially putting Oscar through further surgery that might not work and that would cause him more pain.

'Who are we doing this for Mike, is it for us or for Oscar?'

'Kate, you know I'd only want what is right for the boy.'

Mike was right. He is a big man, tall and built like a prop forward, but he was the kindest, most gentle man I'd ever met. He would be the first to help anyone in need at any time. He would collect me when I went out with my friends so I didn't have to take a taxi, he would collect the children from wherever they were and take them back to their mother's at any time of day and night. He helped friends move house; he was twenty-four-hour helpdesk support for all the family's computer problems (his day job is working in IT in a bank—not as a bank manager which has sometimes been reported). There was nothing he would not do for other people (although, to be honest, he rarely did any housework and he was still thinking about whether 'procrastination' was his middle name or not). He also loved the cats to the extreme. Each morning I would feed the cats a random pouch or tin of cat food, grabbed from the cupboard. At teatime, Mike would check with me which flavour they had had, so he didn't duplicate. I soon learned to check the flavour, as he seemed taken aback if I didn't remember. 'It was the rabbit one. Or it might have been turkey,' I'd say, although I was pretty sure they all tasted the same. They all looked the same, in various shades of pink with brown viscous gravy over the meat (our cats treated this like a starter of soup, as they licked it all off first before biting into the so-called tasty morsels). He became increasingly concerned about the type of cat food we were feeding the cats. He checked the meat content of one of the proprietary brands of cat food.

'Did you know there is only four per cent meat in this?' he commented looking at the pouch.

'That's terrible considering they're meant to be carnivores!' he continued. I must admit I hadn't taken a great deal of notice, but he did have a point and consequently we now try to get food from the pet shop with a much higher percentage of meat or fish—upwards of 50–75 per cent. Mike also cooks the cats' hot meals every evening, usually chicken or fish, which we buy in bulk from the frozen food shop and on Sundays, and if they've been good, they have a tin of tuna. Each night they also get a bowl of special cat milk.

He was also thoughtful about the cats' environment. I couldn't understand why the metal mud-scraping mat was not properly aligned to our front door. It had puzzled me for months, but I had never really questioned why it was off-centre. One day Mike saw me moving it to a more central position and he said, 'I move it so the cats don't hurt their paws when they come in through the cat flap.' Something that had never even crossed my mind.

Today, though, was not about the other cats. It was all about Oscar. Truth be told, we were both ambivalent. Of course we wanted Oscar to live more than anything, but we wanted him to have a happy full life too. We wondered if we'd be taking too much away from him if we went ahead. On the other hand, not going ahead would take everything away from him.

We asked Peter more questions. We wanted to know if Oscar would still be able to live the life he'd had until now. We were particularly keen to know if he would still be able to go outside. He had loved being an outdoor cat and although it would have been a lot safer for him if he had been an indoor cat, we believed he would have missed out on the enriching life that he had had to date.

Peter was realistic and reminded us there was a long way to go before things like that could even be considered. He checked with Noel and the consensus was that there was no reason why Oscar shouldn't be an outdoor cat as he was before, however, as Noel also reiterated, that was still a considerable way off. It was a comfort to us. To keep him inside, when the other three cats enjoyed the right to roam and come and go as they pleased, seemed cruel.

We wondered what Oscar would have wanted if he could decide for himself. He had shown such bravery and tenacity in the past we were pretty sure he would want to go ahead with the operation. Or maybe we were just trying to convince ourselves that he would as we were taking that decision for him.

*   *   *

We were under no illusion that the road ahead would be easy. We knew it was long and uncharted. We weren't even sure if the operation was going to be viable. I finally got to talk to Noel the following weekend.

'Hi there, I've had a look at his pictures and he looks like a suitable candidate,' he said in his smooth Irish tones, 'but until I see the little fella for myself, I can't say that we'll definitely be able to go ahead.'

Noel explained that the fact that the operation had never been done on a double amputee would mean that Oscar would be the first in the world and, of course, being first means there's no precedent, no statistics of success rates and therefore, to a large degree, it was experimental.

Nonetheless, Noel filled us with confidence. His passion was almost tangible. We could tell that he wanted it to work and he would do whatever it took to make the operation a success. He told us of the potential risks: the implants might not take, infection either pre- or post-operative or complications during surgery. It did seem an awful lot to be putting Oscar through.

'The thing is,' said Noel in his matter-of-fact way, 'if you don't do it, you'll have no cat anyway.' He was right; this was Oscar's only hope of survival. He could not walk around on bandaged stumps indefinitely.

Whilst Noel and Peter continued to liaise, Mike and I talked of almost nothing else. Were we doing the right thing? Was it right for Oscar? Who were we to put him through what would be undoubtedly a great deal more pain for him. Indeed, a potentially huge amount of pain. Some might say, he was only a cat, but did we, as his owners, have that right ethically or morally to make that decision? Or should we give him a chance of life? Was it right to put him to sleep when this amazing opportunity had presented itself?

We made our decision. The next dilemma was the logistics of getting Oscar to England. He was recovering well from his accident, in so much as his stumps were healing over and he was bright and perky. Every time we went to visit him, seeing his little face, we were further reassured that the decision to proceed was the right one. He did a little 'meow' and looked excited when we went into New Era to see him. He didn't seem ready to leave this earth yet.

Over in England, Noel was working closely with a team from University College London who were making Oscar's implants. Until these were ready, the operation couldn't go ahead. This entailed detailed liaison between all the parties involved as the precision sizing had to be exactly right to a hundredth of a millimetre.

Whilst we were waiting for Noel to give us the green light to take Oscar over to England, something unexpected happened. We were allowed to take Oscar home. We had been uncertain about whether he'd ever see our house again, so we were delighted to put him into his green cat carrier and bring him back.

He didn't exactly receive a hero's welcome from his sisters. Lou and Buzz sniffed him with indifference and Poppy hissed and exited stage left as quickly as she could. We should have known by now this was the reaction he would receive on his return. It did seem to us that none of the cats missed Oscar when he was having one of his many visits to the vet. He had already spent about eight weeks out of the last two years as an inpatient and it seemed that once he was gone for a day or two the other cats just assumed he was not coming back, and when he did, they treated him like a stranger.

Oscar bumbled round the lounge checking out what had changed in the couple of weeks he'd been away. He was walking better on his bandages (he was now sporting bright pink ones with smiley faces). His back legs were still splayed out and he had trouble getting them onto the floor where he wanted them, but he was fast around the room. His curiosity also remained undiminished. He sniffed round the fireplace, tried to get into the under-stair cupboard to see if there was anything new and exciting in it, and checked out the food activity in the kitchen. He was behaving exactly like he had always done. At night we put him to bed in the spare room, away from the temptation of the cat flap. This was Rachael's room but as she was away at university her bed was not needed for now. We bought a lovely soft cat bed for Oscar, which we placed on the floor by the radiator. Yes, another cat bed. We thought that this one had a particular softness to it that the ones languishing in the loft did not. He was bound to like this one, particularly as his restricted mobility meant that he had to live life at ground level for the time being.

'He'll be fine there,' I said to Mike. 'He's got a bowl of biscuits, water and a litter tray. He'll be good there till morning.' No sooner had we shut the door than he started scratching it.

'Go to sleep,' I called.

'Meow, meow, meow,' came his plaintive voice, which was hard to ignore. I went to check on him. All he wanted was a head nuzzle and a bit of fuss. Maybe I should have read him a bedside story.

The next morning I went to let him out but he wasn't in his bed on the floor. I looked around under the dressing table and behind the bed. He wasn't there. Panic flashed through my mind. If he had pushed the door open and gone downstairs he could have gone through the cat flap. Had I not shut the door properly last night? Was the door ajar when I had gone in just now? I didn't think so, but was I sure? Then I saw a black, furry cat having a languorous stretch on the bed. How many times did we need to be told a human bed would always take precedence over a cat bed?

'Oscar! How did you get up there?' I asked somewhat incredulously.

I didn't know whether to be worried or pleased that he was springing up from his bandaged back legs. I settled for the latter, although I wasn't entirely sure he was meant to be jumping about the place.

After a few days at home he seemed relaxed and all we had to do now was wait for the call from Noel to say we could take him over to England. We were not sure when this would be, but we anticipated getting the call in a couple of days. In the meantime, we took Oscar to New Era every other day to have his dressings changed. He hated seeing his cat carrier and as soon as it made an appearance he tried to hide.

One evening we put him in the bedroom at the end of the day and not long after we had gone to bed we heard him cry out. It wasn't his usual, 'Give me a bit of love, Mummy' meow. It was a call that needed attention. Once again, I didn't see Oscar as I went into the room, but I did see blood. There were dots of blood in a line on the carpet that led me to the end of the bed, where Oscar was cowering. One of his bandages had come off and he was bleeding. It was the first time I had seen his stump and my stomach churned. Because his bandages had been shaped to look like artificial feet (for practical rather than aesthetic purposes) it was a shock to see for myself the magnitude of the battle he faced.

'Mike, ring the vet's, we need to take him down,' I shouted down the stairs. 'They will have to put his bandages on again.' This was not something we could do at home. It required the specialist skills of the nurses and vet.

We got in the car and once again made the journey to New Era Veterinary Hospital that we'd made on so many occasions. We were let in at the side door and handed Oscar over to Ollie, the duty vet. I'm surprised we didn't have our own key.

He took a look at Oscar and scratched his head, 'I'm going to take him round the back to have a look. Can you guys wait out here for moment?'

We flicked through a magazine on the table in the dim, deserted reception area. It was almost more shop than waiting room. We were surrounded by mountains of pet food for every variant of dog or cat you could imagine—neutered small dog, giant puppies (whatever they were), sensitive dog, fussy dog, kidney conditions, long-haired cats, short-haired cats, indoor cats, outdoor cats, fur ball sensitive—you name it, there was a type food for it.

'I wonder what the chances of Oscar making it to "Senior" food are,' mused Mike as we waited for Ollie to bring Oscar back through. Then we heard a loud, distressed-sounding 'meow'.

'That was Oscar,' said Mike and we looked at each other, both concerned that he might have hurt himself further having walked around on his unbandaged stump.

Although New Era is the largest veterinary practice in the Channel Islands and offers a twenty-four-hour emergency service, on the occasions we had been there late at night, there were rarely any other animals waiting to be seen. This time, just after Oscar arrived, a couple with a black dog in their arms turned up and were let in by the nurse.

'So you reckon he drank it in the last hour?' the nurse asked as they handed the dog over to her.

'Yes, we think so,' replied an anxious-looking woman in her mid thirties.

'Ollie's been on the phone to toxicology, so I'll take him through.'

The distraught-looking couple took a seat in the waiting room. Mike and I looked at each other. We understood that his urgent treatment would take precedence over Oscar's re-bandaging.

Ollie came out to the waiting room. He was tall and gangly and looked more like a surfer than a vet; not that all vets wander around looking like James Herriot in tweed jackets and green wellies, of course.

'Do you know what type of paint thinner it was?' he asked the couple.

'It was just some stuff from B&Q. It was outside

107

the back door and we saw him taking a few laps of it,' replied the concerned man.

'OK, I'm just waiting for a call back from the hospital and I'll let you know what's what as soon as we can.'

I'd never really considered before how human medical and veterinary practitioners would help each other.

Ollie came over to us.

'Sorry guys, I'm going to have to sedate Oscar to rebandage him. Peter can do it without sedation, but Oscar's not used to me. The best thing is for us to keep him tonight and you can pick him up in the morning.'

'Thanks Ollie, that's fine. We'll leave you to it. Thanks again.'

Off we went leaving Oscar once more at his home from home.

We picked him up the next morning with his new bandages, bright green with smiley faces this time. Luckily he hadn't caused any further damage to his stump.

'That colour's good on him!' Mike said as he took Oscar in his cat carrier from the nurse. 'Do you know how that dog is by any chance?' Mike continued. 'The one that was poisoned?'

'He's doing as well as can be expected. We think he's going to be fine,' assured the nurse.

CHAPTER 10

GETTING TO ENGLAND

Whilst work on Oscar's implants was underway in England, we had to decide whether to take Oscar to the UK by boat or plane. We soon ruled out crossing by sea. Oscar had not travelled more than five miles in one go in his life and being autumn, a time when the weather can be inclement and gales not unlikely, we thought it was not the best time of year to see if he had sea legs. He was short of legs as it was. The cross channel fast ferry takes about three hours from Jersey, so if it was choppy it could be a long and unpleasant journey.

One day when we were at New Era getting Oscar's bandages changed, Peter gave us a list of private pilots who might be willing to fly Oscar over. We had a slight problem in that we could not give them a precise date. We tried a few, but people were either busy as half term was coming up, or otherwise occupied. One kind man did offer to take him, but he was only available before Noel would have been ready for him. We could not take him over until the implants were finished. Noel's practice, Fitzpatrick Referrals, is based at Godalming in Surrey so the nearest airport is Gatwick. It looked like it was going to be British Airways for Oscar as the other commercial carrier to Gatwick did not take pets at that time of year because they do not heat the hold. It's amazing the things you learn.

Five weeks after the accident, the call came. The

implants were ready and Noel was ready to do the operation. Oscar was ready to travel. We went to New Era to collect the paperwork that Peter had provided which we needed for both the airline and also for Noel.

The nurses and office staff packed some treats for him; some biscuits, Feliway to calm him on the journey, and one of his favourite toys, a hoggy.

We did think, however, that it was unwise to give Oscar a hoggy, as he did not have any back paws which are essential in the destruction process. However, we were reassured not to worry by the nurses at the vet's, and so we bought another hoggy, which would be his teddy when he went on the plane.

Booking a plane ticket for a cat proved to be considerably more complicated than that for a human. We agreed that Mike would take him across and I would stay at home and look after the other cats with the help of Mike's son Chris. Oscar had to go 'animal cargo', which sounded industrial and unpleasant and was also very expensive. A one-way ticket was in the region of £600 for Oscar and a return ticket for Mike was £110. This for a flight of around forty minutes' duration. Oscar wouldn't be getting any cabin service or the opportunity to buy duty-free catnip either. The flight was booked for the Thursday morning and Oscar had to be at the airport three hours before departure.

We put him into his cat carrier (which we had taken to the airport the previous night to get clearance that it was appropriate for travel) and lined his box with newspaper and a blanket. We bought a rabbit's water bottle to attach to the outside of the carrier and placed the little hoggy next to him.

'You're going on a big adventure, Oscar. You're going to see a special vet who is going to do everything he can to make you better. You're going on an aeroplane that will be noisy and might make you feel a bit funny, but Daddy will meet you at the other end,' I tried to reassure Oscar, knowing my words were meaningless but hoping my tone was soothing. I waved them off, thinking that it could be the very last time I saw Oscar.

'Good luck. Be brave,' I said not sure if I was really addressing Mike or Oscar; I choked back my tears as they went down the drive into the great unknown. Oscar had no idea what lay ahead of him. It was probably just as well.

Mike dropped Oscar off at the Animal Reception Centre near the airport. We'd put 'This Way Up' stickers on his cat carrier, which we hoped would be superfluous and we'd also stuck a letter to the box explaining that it contained an injured cat. Two hours later Mike boarded the plane hoping that Oscar was comfortable in the hold below. As the plane raced down the runway and took off, Mike wondered what Oscar would be making of the new sensations he would be experiencing and pondered if he would be as frightened as some human passengers can be. He would obviously not be concerned with the fact the plane might crash or that there might be catastrophic engine failure, however he would be experiencing bodily sensations that could cause him distress. There was nothing Mike could do about it. Luckily the flight itself was short and smooth, and Mike hurried through the airport to pick up the hire car. It seemed to take forever for them to check utility bills, driving licence, time of return and then the obligatory check of the vehicle. Half an hour later, Mike was on his way to the Animal Reception Centre on the outskirts of Gatwick Airport.

'I've come to pick up my cat from flight BA8036 from Jersey,' Mike told the man on reception. The place was not dissimilar to a Post Office parcels collection point.

'Take a seat. We're just checking the paperwork,' he replied.

Mike sat down and waited. Although Jersey is not part of the UK, thankfully there are no quarantine restrictions, although clearly all animals being brought into the country have to be checked. Mike was not sure specifically which paperwork was being checked. Oscar did not require a passport under the Pet Travel Scheme and the fact that the forwarding address on his box was a veterinary practice may have suggested there was a medical condition that required attention. Nevertheless, the only real option for Mike was to drink the bitter machine coffee and wait. It took two hours to be cleared through the system. Oscar seemed to have come out unscathed from the flight; what he made of it we will never know.

Mike put Oscar in the car and drove the half-hour journey to Eashing, just outside Godalming, to meet Oscar's potential saviour. A long, private lane leads you to a large, timber-clad building that is home to one of the most state-of-the-art veterinary practices in the world.

Fitzpatrick Referrals is set in beautiful Surrey countryside and on the approach you can see the low-level building surrounded by open farmland.

112

Noel Fitzpatrick, who has established the most advanced and innovative diagnostic surgical and rehabilitation facilities for dogs and cats in the UK, wanted to create a place that was conducive to ensuring the animals had the most comfortable stay possible. He has a 'no bars' policy, so each 'room' on the wards is enclosed with reinforced glass. This can be written on and is used as a 'quick reference' guide. The walls and floor coverings are bacteria-resistant with underfloor heating, and air conditioning is optimised with high-efficiency particulate air filtering to minimise the possibility of infection. Each kennel has a radio and many of the larger ones have an inbuilt flat-screen TV. Dimmer switches are used to make a more natural night and day setting.

Noel is one of those extraordinary people who, once he enters your life, becomes a huge part of it. Charismatic and passionate, with a huge empathy for pet owners ('Mums and Dads' as he calls us), he also has a highly technical brain; he's a mercurial mix of softness and science.

Born in Mountmellick, near Portlaoise in Ireland in 1970 and growing up on a farm, he knew he wanted to be a vet from a young age. Having qualified from University College Dublin in 1990, he undertook scholarships at the University of Pennsylvania in the USA and the University of Ghent in Belgium. After spending several years in practice in Dublin and England, he founded Fitzpatrick Referrals in 1997 and moved to their current premises of converted farm buildings in 2008. The facility was opened by DJ Chris Evans, whose German Shepherd dog, Enzo, had been treated by Noel.

In an interview with Chris Harvey of *The Daily Telegraph* in November 2010, Noel described his typical day as consulting from 9 a.m. to 12.30 p.m., then operating from 1 p.m. to midnight. He then spends an hour online talking to students; he is Assistant Professor at the University of Florida School of Veterinary Medicine and Visiting Professor at the University of Surrey. He says he survives on four to four-and-a-half hours' sleep a night. He has a passion for both learning and teaching and in 2011 he launched the Fitzpatrick Learning Academy, an online facility for veterinary professionals. The programme offers users a compelling, engaging and interactive learning experience—a world in which nurses can learn, share, empower one another through the development of social networks and ultimately, equip themselves with the skills and the knowledge to deliver the very best in patient care.

In 2010 Noel Fitzpatrick set up 'Fitzpatrick Education Foundation', a non-profit organisation which provides resources for educating future veterinary surgeons and nurses, who may not otherwise have been able to afford such education.

We had agreed with Noel to undertake any publicity surrounding Oscar, in lieu of a large amount of the cost of the operation. A film crew greeted Mike at Fitzpatrick Referrals. He was prepared for this as Noel had advised him they would be filming the last part of the TV series *The Bionic Vet*. Noel said Oscar might not make it onto the final cut of the programme as it was the tail end of filming, which had taken place over the previous two years. Mike donned his favourite shirt and gave the signature front spikes of his dark hair an extra slick of gel to ensure it was not a flop. Jim Incledon, the filmmaker, was poised with the camera as Noel came out to meet Mike.

'Michael, I'm Noel,' Noel offered his hand. 'We haven't even spoken on the phone!' It was true, I had spoken to Noel a few weeks previously, but nearly all liaisons had been between Peter and Noel directly. Noel cut a dashing figure; tall, lithe with a delightful Irish lilt. He looked inside Oscar's box and introduced himself.

'Hey mate!' he greeted Oscar, giving him a stroke through the bars of his box.

'So Michael, tell me what happened.'

Mike recounted the story of the accident for the benefit of the TV crew as Noel knew the series of events only too well.

They then moved through to one of the many consulting rooms so Oscar could be examined. It was still not totally confirmed that Noel would undertake the operation and, despite receiving case notes and X-rays, he wanted to check first-hand that the operation would be viable.

Noel took Oscar out of the box—some seven hours after he was first put in it—and sitting cross-legged on the floor, gave him a cuddle.

'Cats walk on their toes,' Noel explained to Mike. 'He only has his ankles.'

He demonstrated where the break was on his own shoeless, stripy-socked feet. 'He has nothing below. Basically, either we put new feet on him or we have to put him to sleep.'

Noel explained how the radical surgery would work. He had been working with two engineers from University College London who had made the implants. This would be the first time such implants

115

had been used in an ankle, let alone in two. Oscar would be the first cat in the world to have this.

Oscar sat gently in Noel's arm, sniffing the unfamiliar environment.

'He's so sweet isn't he?' cooed Noel. It seemed such a contradiction that this man could be so scientifically minded, such a pioneering surgeon and yet be bowled over by our little moggy.

Oscar snuggled up more closely.

'My goodness, that's why it would be unbearable to put him to sleep. He's such a character isn't he? He's so full of life. He's tolerated all this so well. He's unbelievably calm.' Oscar was. He lay comfortably in Noel's arms, unperturbed by a stranger holding him.

'I very rarely see cats like this,' said Noel. 'Normally they'd be trying to claw my eyes out.'

It was love at first sight for both of them.

Noel, however, was quick to point out his concerns. He told Mike his three main worries were skin breakdown, bone breakdown and infection. 'I'll do my very best,' he assured Mike, who was in no doubt that he would.

After a few minutes completing various consent forms for the operation, Mike said goodbye to Oscar, leaving his fate in Noel's hands. He had done all he could for the time being. With a heavy heart, but also a sense of optimism, he headed back to Jersey.

CHAPTER 11

THE SCIENCE BIT

The implants Noel was going to put into Oscar's legs used a technique which effectively grew with the bone ensuring a fully integrated implant. Metal and bone would fuse together. A small titanium rod, coated in hydroxyapatite (a major component of bones and teeth that gives them their rigidity) would poke through the skin, allowing prosthetics to be attached to this rod.

Risk of infection, which could be caused by bacteria passing from the external limb through the rod to the bone, is avoided because the skin tissue meshes around the rod to form a seal.

To work out how to attach live tissue directly to metal, scientists from the Centre for Biomedical Engineering, UCL (University College London), led by Professor Gordon Blunn and Dr Catherine Pendegrass, looked at how deer's antlers grow through the animals' skin without infection. Professor Blunn has extensive experience in orthopaedic medical devices, materials and musculo-skeletal tissues and has led many successful research projects, funded by government bodies and orthopaedic companies. He has also established a team of dynamic researchers, some of whom are focused on enhancing massive endoprosthetic replacements, in other words, implants that are inserted into the body, which is what Oscar would be having.

Noel was liaising constantly with Professor Blunn

regarding Oscar's implants and had previously used this type of implant on a dog called Coal. The dog had cancer in his wrist and arthritis in his knee so, had the alternative of amputation taken place, he would have struggled to survive with three legs. As his cancer was a slow-growing type, an implant was thought to give him the best option of a normal life. The operation was a success and Coal went on to lead a pain-free, active life, using his prosthetic paw for knocking at the door and his natural paw for playing with toys.

Although Noel was not the first to use an osseointegrated limb (live bone growing into a surgical implant), Oscar was the first cat to have two limbs fitted simultaneously. It was also the first time these specific types of implants were successfully used in two weight-bearing bones, allowing for movement in the adjacent joint.

A cat called George Bailey had been the first cat to have a successfully integrated prosthetic limb. Dr Denis Marcellin-Little undertook the operation in March 2005 at the North Carolina State University's College of Veterinary Medicine. Dr Marcellin, a professor of orthopaedics, and Dr Ola Harrysson, an associate professor of industrial and systems engineering at NC State, developed a pioneering 'rapid prototyping' process to aid in the development and customisation of missing limbs and the creation of titanium implants that fuse living bone with specially designed prosthetic limbs. Since George Bailey, the team has successfully completed the process with another cat—Mr Franz—as well as several dogs. Engineering, 3-D prototyping, custom computer-generated implantable body parts surgery, and follow-up medical monitoring on patients have been completed at NC State.

As Noel reminded us, there was a significant difference between doing a single implant and doing a double. We were well aware that if the operation did not work, then we would have to say goodbye to Oscar. We never asked ourselves what would happen if one implant worked and one did not. We were living each day at time, never trying to look too far ahead.

Noel told us he would operate once Oscar was settled and they had managed to get rid of an infection he had in one of his stumps. He had picked up *E. coli*, probably from the field at the time of the accident. This bacterium is notoriously hard to treat, and Noel and his team were managing the amount of antibiotics they were administering very carefully. Such was the magnitude of the operation they could not afford to take risks. All we could do was wait.

On Friday 13 November 2009, Noel rang Mike to say he had performed the operation and it had been a success. It had lasted three hours and had required the most delicate of touches, as Noel had drilled into each ankle. The hole for the implant needed to be quite big but the ankle bone was very small. With the greatest precision and with not a millimetre margin for error possible, Noel focused on one of his most challenging cases. The TV crew were in the room filming for *The Bionic Vet* and we later learnt it was all they could do to keep concentrating and not look away—it was a very gory operation and the sound of the drill going into Oscar's legs made even the strongest stomach lurch.

When the ankles had been hollowed out, Noel carefully inserted the implant. Again this was a delicate procedure as there was a real risk that the bone would be split with the insertion. Once the implants were safely in place, the final stage of the procedure was to stitch the skin around it. The tendons supply blood to the skin to form a bond, leaving the point of the implant sticking out so the prosthetic foot can be attached once the healing has taken place.

Noel and his team constructed Meccano-like metal frames which were attached around both feet to prevent Oscar from standing and putting weight on them until he had healed. Although the operation had gone as well as could be anticipated, there were still many hurdles ahead. His body could reject the implants or his skin might fail to bond effectively. The risk of infection was high, but for now everything was as good as could be hoped for.

On the day of the operation, I was in London for the weekend staying with my sisters, Elizabeth and Victoria. Every year the three of us get together on our own, without husbands/partners or children, and have a weekend to ourselves. This weekend we had planned a trip to Kensington Palace and the obligatory shopping expedition.

On the Friday night I received a text from Mike saying the operation had taken place. I was taken aback that it had happened without me knowing, but at the same time, pleased that I had not spent the whole day worrying about it.

'That's fantastic news!' exclaimed Elizabeth. 'Are you still going to go and see him?'

I had already arranged with Noel to see him on the Sunday morning on my way to the airport.

As I was in England it made sense for me to visit Oscar, although when planning this the previous week, I didn't know he would have already had his operation. I rang Noel the next morning to confirm my approximate time of arrival and to establish where exactly to meet him. The practice was closed to the public on Sunday, other than for people visiting their pets by appointment, and so the doors would be locked.

It was all sorted. I would leave my sister Elizabeth's house in Beaconsfield, take the train to London and then another one down to Godalming, changing at Guildford. From there I would take a taxi for the three miles to Fitzpatrick Referrals in Eashing. I could stay for an hour and a half then I would to head to Gatwick, in time for my afternoon flight. Victoria and I double-checked the train times and I was all set for Sunday. In the meantime, my sisters and I boarded the train to Marylebone for our day out in the capital. A little later as we were walking through the gardens of Kensington Palace, we tried to imagine where Princess Diana's quarters had been as we approached the magnificent red-brick building. We marvelled at her dresses displayed in an exhibition at the Palace and walked through magnificent rooms admiring the paintings and learning the history of the building. Our tour was not all historic though; we stumbled on a fun interactive exhibition too, where you could practice curtseying in front of a mirror, following the detailed instructions. We giggled our way round before finishing our trip in The Orangery, a magnificent glass structure which was built in the eighteenth century for Queen Anne and had been home to much court entertainment.

121

We treated ourselves to an afternoon tea of dainty finger sandwiches and freshly baked scones with clotted cream and jam. Despite living mainly in Devon, I noticed my sister Elizabeth favoured the Cornish way of eating them with jam on first then cream on top. In Devon the reverse prevails and there is much banter between the two counties as to which is the correct way. High on sugar and carbs we walked back across Kensington Gardens as the sun disappeared from the sky and an autumn chill wrapped itself around us.

Then I received a phone call from Noel.

'I've been thinking about it and I don't think it's a good idea for you to see him yet,' he said. 'It's still very early days after the operation and it's probably not for the best. He won't look how you'll expect.'

I was distraught. I desperately wanted to see him, regardless of how he looked. The last time I'd seen Oscar was nearly a month ago when he had left the house to catch the plane.

'Please Noel, the thing is I don't know when I'll next be in England. Even if I stay just for a few minutes?' Noel paused for a moment. He was clearly not happy that I should see him so soon.

'Honestly, it's for your own sake. He's doing fine but it's still early days,' he continued.

I pleaded again and somewhat reluctantly he agreed I could visit, but he warned me again to be prepared for what I would see. I knew he had my best interests at heart.

'It can't be that bad,' said Victoria. She worked in the medical profession and was a lot more used to seeing shocking things than I was.

'I'm sure it won't be as bad as when his bandage fell off and his stump was bleeding!' I replied. I was trying to imagine what would be so horrific that Noel wanted to shield me from it. I would have to wait until the next day.

Much later that evening, after a meal at a Moroccan restaurant, we crawled into bed. Since our beloved father died in 2007, every time we have a weekend together we always share the same bedroom. We talk late into the night and laugh at things no one else would find the slightest bit funny, but to us it is like medicine. We always feel so much better the next day. That night, though, all I could think about was Oscar.

* * *

The next morning I left Beaconsfield Station and caught the 9.50 a.m. train to Marylebone, where I jumped into a taxi and crossed London, which always seems so different on a Sunday. It was a fine day and people were out walking, taking in the sights and even the air seemed fresher and cleaner than it does on a weekday. At Waterloo Station I grabbed a bagel, knowing I was unlikely to eat until I got to Gatwick later that afternoon. I caught a train down to Guildford and then changed onto a branch line for the ten-minute train journey to Godalming. Not having trains in Jersey, I particularly enjoy this form of travel. Jersey did once have a railway service but the last passengers travelled on it in 1936 and whilst you can see remnants of it (The Railway Walk is popular with both walkers and cyclists and The Old Station Café is just what it sounds like), it is very much defunct. I arrived at Godalming bang on time at 12.40 p.m. and I had until 2.03 p.m. before I had to get the train onwards to Gatwick Airport.

I emerged from the train station, which was much smaller than I had expected, and headed to the taxi office across the road.

'Can I help you, Miss?' asked a very cheerful man as he hobbled around on a bad leg.

'Please can I go to Fitzpatrick Referrals?'

'I haven't got anything for a good hour I'm afraid.'

Disaster! I hadn't factored in this outcome.

'Oh no!' I exclaimed. 'I've come all the way from Jersey to see my cat and I've only got an hour and a half!' With hindsight, that did sound a little implausible and ever so slightly melodramatic.

'I'm really sorry, but Terry has got a family birthday lunch, Margaret has got a Heathrow job and Gerry's on holiday,' he said sympathetically.

'Are there any other firms?' I asked, almost in tears by now. Why hadn't I pre-booked a taxi? What a stupid oversight.

'No, we're the only one I'm afraid love. Let me have a think.'

'How far is it to walk?' I asked, ignoring the fact I had a suitcase, albeit a small one, plus two shopping bags with me.

'Too far, I reckon,' he replied. By now he was flicking through an ancient Rolodex and picking up the phone.

'Derek, Stan here. You're not available for a station to Eashing job are you?'

The look on Stan's face whilst Derek replied told me all I needed to know.

'OK, thought I'd just check,' said Stan despondently.

Stan must have called about five or six different drivers, none of whom were available. I wondered if he would take me himself, but looking at his gammy leg I thought he might not have been able to drive at all. Maybe I would have to hitch a lift for the first time in my life.

'You can? That's marvellous. See you in a few minutes.'

Stan had good news. I was so grateful I wanted to throw my arms him. Without a doubt he had gone way beyond the call of duty to help a damsel in distress. I felt like nominating him for a Pride of Britain award.

The driver soon turned up and I felt the stress drain from my body.

'He's an incredible vet,' the taxi driver told me as he recounted how Noel had treated his friend's dog's back with great success.

When we arrived he offered to come back and collect me after an hour. I hadn't even thought about the return journey. For a competent, capable woman there were some serious gaps in my ability to think ahead.

I was a little confused as to where to meet Noel. He had said to go to reception and wait outside the door. There seemed to be two receptions, one on either side of the large building, and I couldn't work out which one was which, being that they were both in darkness. I rang the number, but it was diverted to an answerphone, advising that they were currently shut. Boldly, I pushed one of the doors and found it unlocked. I went in, there was no one there so I looked around and saw there was a staircase.

I shouted out to see if anyone came. No one did, so I started to climb the stairs.

'Hello, is anyone there?' I repeated.

'Hi, sorry about that, I didn't realise you were here.'

I recognised the voice immediately. In front of me stood Noel Fitzpatrick, an extraordinarily good-looking man, around six feet tall with eyelashes that most women would pay a lot of good money for.

'It's so good to meet you at last!' I exclaimed.

He shook my hand and I could almost feel the charisma leaking out of him. In his consulting room he outlined the surgery Oscar had undergone and showed me on a model skeleton exactly where the implants were. I was rather overwhelmed with all the science he explained to me, particularly as I was finding him so distracting. The man was clearly a genius. I was so busy concentrating on his total coolness, that I couldn't possibly be expected to take in everything he said.

'I'm going to get Oscar now. Are you sure you're ready?' asked Noel.

'Yes, definitely,' I assured him, composing myself.

'OK, well, like I said yesterday, I wouldn't usually want you to see him in this state, so brace yourself.'

He disappeared for a few minutes, giving me a chance to take in the surroundings. The consulting rooms are cleverly designed with a door on one side leading to the waiting room and a door on the other side leading to the clinical areas. There was a walk-on set of scales inserted into the floor, which meant cats and dogs would not have to climb up on to them. As well as the examination table, there was also a desk with a PC and an X-ray viewer. It was all very slick and modern.

Noel brought Oscar through in his arms and

126

laid him on a furry rug on the examination table. I braced myself as instructed.

'Hello boy,' I said. He looked up and made a small mewing noise.

I could see why Noel had prepared me. Oscar's hind legs had been shaved and whilst I had seen one of his stumps before, seeing both of them exposed with the metal of the implant poking through and congealed blood around them, was not for the faint-hearted. Perhaps worse than that from a layperson's point of view were the metal frames which surrounded his legs. These were essential to allow healing and to prevent Oscar from putting any weight on his new implants. Some of the metal had been bound in soft material and covered in black polythene for comfort and protection. They looked cumbersome and heavy. He had a big Elizabethan collar around his neck to prevent him licking and I wondered how he could possibly groom himself. The worst thing, though, was not being able to tell Oscar it was part of the process to make him better. He purred when I stroked him, but I'd read that purring could be brought on by stress as well as pleasure. Thoughts whirled through my head. We had gone too far. We should never have put him through this, the poor little chap. He'd survived all the trauma just so we could have our pet. I wondered if we had been selfish in the extreme. Whether it had all been a terrible mistake; an experiment too far.

Both Mike and I had agreed from the beginning that we only wanted to do what was best for Oscar, and did not want to do what was best for the vet or for us. Noel agreed with this sentiment. He said he did not operate or undertake procedures because he could; he did it where he thought he should. Seeing Oscar had made me question my judgment. Surely it was one thing having a human go through this sort of procedure where they knew what the outcome would be, but an entirely different situation for an animal who had no say or control over what was happening to its body. For the first time I regretted what we'd done. I felt I had no right to make Oscar go through this procedure. We had all been wrong.

'Oscar really wants to live. He's got real fight in him,' Noel said, second-guessing my concerns.

Oscar was the least likely cat to get into a fight or to scratch or hiss; yet his determination to come through his operation and not give up was clear to see. He was as gentle as a little kitten but he had nerves of steel. And legs of titanium now.

I took a few pictures of his implants and of his little face to show Mike later. I gently stroked him and told him what a brave little chap he was.

'It'll all be worth it,' I whispered to him gently as I tickled under his chin. 'You've been through the worst. It won't be long till you're walking again. You're going to get better Osc. It'll be fine.' I could hardly continue. If only he could understand what I was saying. If only he knew. The funny thing was I was starting to believe he did.

I was jolted back from my thoughts when Noel spoke to reiterate that it was very early days and there was still plenty of time for things to go wrong. Although Oscar was one of many animals he worked with, the way he spoke about him made me sense that they were forming a special bond, and for that I was very grateful. For my part, I was having serious misgivings; I felt we had been propelled along a journey over which we had little control. This was not strictly true as we reserved the right at all times to decide on the treatment for Oscar, however, at that moment it felt like we had put him through too much. Mike and I, who loved our animals passionately, were perhaps being too cruel for words. I reminded myself that this was the very reason Noel had not wanted me to see Oscar today. Much the same as a hospital would say no to visitors in the immediate aftermath of extensive surgery; but I had persisted with Noel to be allowed to see Oscar and I should not have at such an early stage. It was too heartbreaking.

The time came for me to go and I thanked Noel for all that he was doing for our little cat. I said goodbye to Oscar who by now was lying comfortably in Noel's arms and went to the taxi, which as promised, had arrived on schedule.

I left Noel and Oscar and returned to the station to head first to Guildford from Godalming, then to Clapham Junction, before arriving at Gatwick at around three o'clock. In the past six hours I had been on six trains and taken three taxis to see Oscar for maybe forty-five minutes. I was glad I had seen him, but I was also very concerned.

CHAPTER 12

LIVING IN ENGLAND

When I got home I told Mike of my fears.

'I really don't think we should have gone ahead. He looked so uncomfortable,' I said to Mike.

'That's why Noel didn't want you to see him. He knew you'd react like this,' he replied.

'I wasn't squeamish about seeing him,' I retorted. 'It just brought it home to me how much he has had to endure, and this is only the beginning.'

'He's been through the worst. He's got the implants now and every day should get a bit better for him,' Mike tried to reassure me. I should have been really happy as we had come such a long way since the day of the accident two months earlier. Instead I felt like we were playing God where we had no right to. Luckily for Oscar, others did not share my view and he continued his recovery at Fitzpatrick Referrals.

We decided to visit him again just before Christmas. The team at New Era Veterinary Hospital were keen to hear how Oscar was getting on and when we said we were going (we tied in the visit with taking over the presents for family in England), asked if we could take over something for Oscar. The nurses had put together a Christmas bag full of toys, snacks, catnip, a Christmas card signed by the staff and of course some hoggies. Oscar appreciated it very much.

As we drove down the lane that leads to Fitzpatrick Referrals we were full of anticipation and excitement. Noel had kept us regularly updated with his progress, but whilst the recovery was generally going well, not everything had gone to plan. We were left in no doubt that Oscar was not out of the woods yet and it was, as we were frequently reminded, still very early days.

Noel greeted us and made us feel like VIP visitors. He fetched Oscar down to one of the consulting rooms and placed him on the floor.

The first thing I noticed was that he no longer had the metal frames round his legs and he was not wearing a collar. He seemed so much better than when I had seen him two days after his operation and we watched with wonder as he walked so much more confidently and purposefully. His gait, which initially was awkward and ungainly, was much better and he seemed pleased to see us revelling in the attention of having two pairs of hands to give him head rubs.

We left after about an hour of sitting on the floor with him and went back to our hotel in Godalming where we would spend the night before returning home the next day. After checking into our room, we decided to go out for a bite to eat. We walked past the quaint little shops, all dressed to the nines in preparation for Christmas and passed the Old Town Hall, nicknamed the Pepper Pot because of its octagonal shape. Marvelling at the beautiful Christmas lights that adorned the streets, we headed towards the ancient parish church of St Peter and St Paul. As we approached the picturesque church (which has appeared in many TV programmes and films) we heard singing emanating from it.

I wished we had arrived a little earlier so we could have gone to the carol service. Neither Mike nor I are particularly religious, but having seen Oscar making such a good recovery, I did wonder if there was someone watching over him and I really did feel like singing.

As it was, we found a restaurant that was serving Sunday roast so settled for that before returning to our room to watch the final of that year's *X Factor*. Poor Mike, he could never get away from that programme no matter where he was.

The next day we chatted about Oscar and both agreed we were delighted with his progress. There were still some misgivings about whether we had done the right thing, but seeing how well he looked had lightened our hearts considerably. On our return to Jersey, we popped down to see his friends at the vet's to give them the update, which of course they were thrilled to hear.

Christmas came and went and we were hopeful that 2010 would be the year Oscar would return to something of a normal life. We also knew, though, that things were not going according to plan for him. Noel had told us that whilst his left implant was acting exactly as it should, he had had to re-operate on the right one as the infection Oscar had picked up at the time of the accident had caused the skin to break down around the site of the implant. We all hoped this operation would solve the problem, but in February we received an email from Noel advising us that despite his best efforts the infection with *Enterococcus* and *E. coli* was still evident and it had flared up in spite of antibiotics after surgery. Noel went on to say that because of this Oscar would have to stay with them so they could monitor him closely and make sure that everything possible was being done to facilitate the healing of the skin around the implant. Noel, in his usual manner of switching from academic scientist to ardent animal lover, rounded off the email by saying that Oscar was getting lots and lots of loving and he wished he could cut off a little bit of Oscar's fur and paste it on himself so he would get more loving from his staff.

We knew that Noel and his team were doing all

they could but nonetheless we were so disappointed that our poor cat had been through so much and was still not out of the woods. How much more could his little body take?

After a lengthy process and restricted use of antibiotics for fear of damaging his kidneys, Oscar's implant was finally infection-free. He continued to improve and was living at Fitzpatrick Referrals for the time being. Noel told us he often sat with Oscar in the evening as he wrote up his notes or scientific papers. We were in no doubt that Oscar was being extremely well cared for but we had no idea when, and indeed if, Oscar would be returning home. We took things day by day and were unsure where his journey was going to lead him. Nor did we have any idea how big his story would become around the world.

*　　　*　　　*

Our next visit to Oscar was in April 2010. We decided to take our car across on the ferry to England, a decision which turned out to be more fortuitous than we could have ever anticipated. At that stage, despite having lived in Jersey for twenty years, I had never returned to England by boat, I always flew. I do enjoy travelling by boat (a trip up the Thames, for example, is, in my mind, one of the most relaxing forms of transport), but I was also very concerned that the weather was often very unpredictable in the English Channel and I was worried that if it got choppy it would be unbearable. I didn't fancy being trapped on a boat with people all around me being sick! Mike pointed out to me the advantages of having our own transport (shopping at John Lewis!) and I surprised myself and agreed that I would give it a try.

We were going to see Oscar on the Monday, but before that we had my stepfather's seventieth birthday party to attend at his and my mum's home in the Cotswolds.

We boarded the boat on the Friday night and it was full to capacity, there was not a spare seat to be had anywhere. The reason was simple. The airport was shut and this was the only means of leaving the island. A couple of days earlier a volcano had erupted in Iceland, spewing a huge cloud of ash. The unpronounceable volcano, Eyjafjallajökull, was wreaking havoc across Europe as airports were closed in the UK, Denmark, Norway, Sweden, Finland, France, Belgium and the Netherlands. Across the world people were stranded, which probably was not too bad if you could not return from your holiday in Barbados, but for many people it was a great inconvenience. For the Jersey ferry company it meant a roaring trade. We spent a very pleasant day on the Saturday sitting in the garden with my mum and stepfather Dick, celebrating his birthday with his three children and our respective families and siblings. My mum, who is an amazing cook, had prepared an enormous feast of cold chicken and ham pie, salads, potatoes and an array of desserts which would have easily made it on to The Savoy sweet menu.

The next day we headed down to stay with friends in South London. I did manage to get some shopping done, including the promised stop at John Lewis. The highlight of the weekend, though, was yet to come. On Monday morning we left the house and made the short journey to Godalming really excited about seeing Oscar for the first time this year. We arrived at about eleven o'clock and took a seat in the waiting room. We had been so used to being 'out of hours' visitors it was unusual for us to see it bristling with activity. Dogs of all shapes and sizes waited patiently (or in some cases, impatiently) with their owners. Some had limps, some had bandages, and some looked fine. All had one thing in common; they had put all their hope and faith in Noel and his remarkable team. The doors of the many consulting rooms were continually opening and closing as a steady stream of patients came and went.

Finally it was our turn and we were guided to one of the rooms whilst a nurse went to fetch Oscar. I felt strangely nervous about seeing him again after all this time. In the meantime Noel came through to update us on Oscar's progress and reassured us he was doing well now the infection was finally clear. He said that the implant on his right foot appeared to be less integrated than the left one, but he was happy that it was now working effectively. He also advised us that, contrary to what we first thought, Oscar would have to be an indoor cat now. This was a disappointment to us. When we embarked on this journey, part of the reason we agreed to it was that we thought Oscar would be able to get his life back to pretty much the same standard as before. With hindsight that view may have been rather naïve. Nonetheless we both felt sad that he was going to have to stay confined within four walls. The nurse brought Oscar in and as ever, he gave a little meow when he saw us. She placed him on the floor and curiosity quickly got the better of him as he began to dart around the room. We were amazed. He was walking so well. He had new blade-like feet and they seemed to allow him to walk almost normally. He was steady and could move at quite a pace.

Mike and I sat on the floor so we could interact with him and he immediately trotted over, sniffing round my handbag, which was by my side. He must have known I had brought some meaty stick treats. I opened the packet to extract one and his mouth was there like a shot. He pulled it out from the foil wrapper and ate it with great delight. The strap of my bag was lying across the floor and as Oscar backed away I was concerned he was going to trip on it. I needn't have worried. Instinctively he knew when to lift his back feet. He walked around the room, going under the desk but not tripping on the wires from the computer. It really was a marvel to behold. He came back over to my handbag and I gave in far too easily and gave him another treat. We spent about half an hour stroking and talking to him and he nuzzled up against us, enjoying the attention. Mike picked him up in his arms and rocked him like a baby whilst Oscar continued to purr.

We were very pleased with his progress. Oscar was not fully recovered but he was definitely well on the way. We left Fitzpatrick Referrals knowing we still had to take each day at a time, but wondering if Oscar would be discharged soon.

CHAPTER 13

THE DAY THE STORY BROKE

We were told the series of *The Bionic Vet* was ready to be broadcast; it was just a question of scheduling it. We were initially advised that it was going to be shown in the spring of 2010, and then we were told it was going to be after the FIFA World Cup, and finally we were told the series was going to be broadcast on BBC One starting on the last Monday in June (which was whilst the World Cup was still on).

The reaction to the press release to promote the broadcast was phenomenal. Although a 'late entry' into the series, Oscar's story, accompanied by a beautiful photograph taken of him by Jim Incledon, the producer and director of the series, made Oscar the focus of the press release. That morning we were woken by the noise on the telephone of texts arriving from friends and family.

'Oscar is on the BBC news!' exclaimed my mum. 'Can't believe it, pic of Oscar in *The Times*,' texted my friend, Jill. Sure enough Oscar's story was in every national newspaper and his story was global within hours of its release. It had appeared on BBC *Breakfast News*, our local ITV station Channel TV, and BBC Channel Islands. For a period of time that morning, his was the most read story on the BBC website. Forums were opening on the web about the miracle of his story. Debates were starting as to whether it was too experimental and cruel. Others thought the cost of the surgery and rehabilitation would have been better spent on care for humans. Overall, though, the majority seemed to marvel at the skill of the surgery and the bravery of our beloved pet. He was being cited as being the human equivalent of Oscar Pistorius, the South African sprint runner and double amputee who runs on two blades. Already our cat was being dubbed as 'Oscar Pawstorius'.

It seemed that no part of the world was untouched by Oscar's story. His moniker has been extended to Oscar the Bionic Cat and googling this brought up literally millions of results. Within days he had his own entry on Wikipedia. He even had his own Facebook page. We have no idea who set these up; they were not created by us or anyone we know. His 'likes' on Facebook continue to go up all the time from people (and curiously from quite a lot of other cats) who have offered many comments of support for our courageous kitty. What was interesting was that nearly every post was directed to Oscar himself. 'Oscar, you are awesome.' 'Oscar, UR the best.' 'Wow, Oscar you're pretty cool.' Humans, it seems, cannot help but anthropomorphise.

Back in the human land, many people were fascinated by the science that had led to the miracle of Oscar's feet. An interview with Noel Fitzpatrick on the *BBC News* summarised the methodology of the process Oscar has been through:

The real revolution with Oscar is [that] we have put a piece of metal and a flange into which skin grows into an extremely tight bone, Fitzpatrick said.

We have managed to get the bone and skin to

grow into the implant and we have developed an "exoprosthesis" that allows this implant to work as a see-saw on the bottom of an animal's limbs to give him effectively normal gait.

Whilst the implants were bedding in, work was underway on Oscar's prosthetic feet. They were being made by Dr Glyn Heath and Geoff Riley from the Prosthetics and Orthotics department of the University of Salford, Manchester. There were certain criteria that had to be met in order to make the feet viable for Oscar. They had to provide him with stability whilst standing, and they needed shock absorption to allow him to walk, run and jump without transmitting excess force through the implants. It was also important to make the back legs as light as possible to ensure Oscar did not to use excessive effort when walking.

Meanwhile, at Fitzpatrick Referrals in their 'gait lab', multiple cameras, linked to a computer, were positioned overlooking a treadmill.

'We analyse the animal's gait here,' explained Noel. 'Cameras pick up movement in three dimensions, we can make models of how an animal moves and then we can predict what force is in it.'

A further challenge of developing the feet was to create each one to be strong enough to withstand everyday stresses yet be able to break ahead of the metal rod in the leg if extraordinary stress was applied, for example if the leg became trapped. The key was to ensure that the metal implant would never break. He and his engineer, Juan Ochoa in Colombia (chosen because the computer modelling required was not available in Britain) spent hours on Skype to develop the feet.

Mike and I had very little experience of the media and were quite unprepared for the level of interest in Oscar. In fact, I had always been rather tongue-tied when speaking to journalists (which I occasionally had to do for my job), which probably arose from my earliest conversation with one when I was eight years old. I was runner-up in a poetry contest, the prize for which was to be an Attendant to the Rose Queen at the inaugural Marlow Bottom Rose Carnival. Standing proudly on the old open-top truck, resplendent in a long pink gown and paper rose coronet, I leaned over to answer the questioning reporter from the local paper. 'What's your name?' she asked. 'Katherine, but Katie for short,' I gabbled. 'Could you repeat that please?' the woman asked. 'Katherine, but Katie for short,' I repeated, even more quickly than before. 'So your surname is Forshort?' This exchange went on for several minutes, until I realised all she wanted was a first name and a surname. The embarrassment totally overshadowed the day for me and made me wary of the media ever since.

Nevertheless, earlier that week Mike and I had done an interview for our local BBC station to tie in a press release which Fitzpatrick Referrals' PR agency had released. The BBC retained all rights to the footage of Oscar walking as they were being used as part of *The Bionic Vet* series, so until it was released on YouTube there was very little that could be shown of him in action. A further problem was that Oscar was not here in Jersey with us. He was still living at Fitzpatrick Referrals whilst he continued to recuperate. When Channel TV rang for an interview, the broadcast coverage was marred by the conspicuous absence of the star of the story—they were only able to use stills of Oscar.

As timing would have it, Mike and I were going to Portugal for our holiday the day the story broke and we were both working till five o'clock. As usual, we had a list of last-minute things to do. Mike still had to pick up his euros and get his toiletries. I had to get a full medicine cabinet's worth of supplies 'just in case', and we also had to pick up Tracey, who would be house-sitting and looking after our three other cats while we were away. The constant phone calls from the PR agency representing Fitzpatrick Referrals made for such a frenetic day that the only job on our 'to do' lists that we managed to achieve was to pick up Tracey. I had to live life on the edge and hope that the airport chemist would be adequately stocked. '*Take a Break* want to run the story,' said Jane, the PR manager. 'Can I give them your number?'

'Yes, that's fine,' answered Mike, 'but we're leaving for Gatwick today, then flying down to Faro first thing in the morning.'

'Hi, it's me again,' said Jane, '*Closer* magazine is interested. I'll get them to call.' The calls kept coming and as we were both at work, we could not take them all. As it was we were both working flat out, at a rate you can only muster when you know you have a fortnight off ahead of you. How efficient the world would be if everyone went on holiday more often! Emails were responded to immediately, clients were called, filing was filed and the best task of all, finally putting the 'Out of Office' signature on. We were ready to go.

The phone calls did not stop, though.

'Hi, do you have any photos of Oscar that *Your Cat* magazine could publish?' asked Jane on her next call a few minutes later.

It was the start of a new world for us. Neither of us had bought cat magazines before, let alone been asked to provide material for them. Mike and I had become known as cat people unwittingly, having four altogether. People were never really comfortable when we said we had four. On the way from the office to the car I popped into the newsagent and there on the front page of our local daily newspaper, the *Jersey Evening Post*, was a picture of Oscar with the caption, 'Meet the world's first bionic cat', with the full story appearing inside headed up, 'Puss in bionic boots'. I bought ten copies. The man in the shop looked at me quizzically. 'That's my cat!' I explained and he smiled.

Mike and I finally got home in the late afternoon and quickly changed, said goodbye to Tracey and to Buzz, Lou and Poppy and raced to the airport. After dropping our bags at the check-in desk, we sat in the bar waiting for our flight to be called. Our respective phones were still ringing constantly.

'We're really interested in Oscar's story,' said one of the representatives from a magazine. 'If you're OK to go ahead, we'll fax you over the contract. It just says you can't speak to any other publications.' This was the general gist of the calls.

We spoke to Jane at the PR company again to get her advice as to what to do for the best. She said that in over thirty years of working she had never had so much interest in a story. When we started this process with Noel Fitzpatrick back in November, we agreed to participate in any publicity that was required on the strict understanding that Oscar's interests would be paramount and his health and well-being would never be compromised. The 'deal' if you like, was we would do any publicity in exchange for Oscar's treatment. It seemed a small price to pay.

Mike and I boarded the plane and looked at each other. Away from the phone calls and frenzy, we could at last draw breath and do something we hadn't really done all day. Speak to each other.

'It's crazy, isn't it?' Mike said.

'Totally,' I replied. 'All this interest in our boy.'

'Let's not do any of the magazines without speaking to Noel.'

'I agree. I don't want Oscar's story to be sensationalised.' Mike agreed with me.

'Especially as his feet are only part of his story,' I said.

A very short forty winks later, we were at Gatwick Airport.

A night at the airport may not be everyone's idea of fun, but we've always loved this part of our holiday because for us, it signals the start of two weeks of bliss. We did not go away for a fortnight every year, which made the times we managed to even more enjoyable. I was apprehensive about going to Portugal, though. I'd been once twenty-odd years previously and partly because of bad weather and partly because I was ill halfway through, I have never had any great desire to return. Mike, however, being half Portuguese, was keen to show me the Algarve. In our four years together I'd managed to steer our holidays to the other side of the Iberian Peninsula, but this time I had agreed to give Portugal a shot.

We gave Tracey a quick call to check that all was well with the cats. As we'd only been gone for about two hours it was unlikely there was much to report.

'You've been on the news!' she excitedly told Mike.

'Was it all right?' he asked, conscious that he was not used to the spotlight.

'You were fine. It was really good,' she replied, adding, 'By the way, Buzz and Lou are asleep and Poppy's in the garden.' No change there then.

'Fine, she said I was fine,' Mike relayed to me, in a voice that suggested that he thought he had been anything but.

'Let's go and find an Internet cafe,' he said, cheering up.

We went across to the North Terminal and found an antiquated (if there could be such a thing) Internet access machine, put our pound coin into the slot, logged on and searched on 'Oscar the Bionic Cat'. There were pages of entries; the story had reached the *New Delhi Times*, the *New Zealand Herald* and the *New York Journal*. We were astounded. Our money only lasted for ten minutes, so we hastily scanned as many sites as we could. We were touched by comments that people had put about what an amazing story it was and how we'd done the right thing. Our little cat that had had the misfortune to be run over by a combine harvester was now having his story shared around the world. All we wanted now was for him to come home.

The Bionic Vet first aired on BBC One on 30 June 2010 and Oscar's operation featured in the first episode. The programme makers, who had been following Noel around for two years, had brilliantly captured the idiosyncrasies of this dedicated and pioneering surgeon. The suggestion on the programme was that Noel frequently slept at the practice and had a bed there. It also showed Noel working morning, noon and night, either directly with patients or preparing papers for the lectures he delivered both in the UK and further afield in Australia or the USA. In our experience this was no exaggeration. He sent us progress updates at four in the morning; he would ring us at eleven-thirty at night. The man never stopped.

On one occasion he explained to us that having borrowed heavily to build the practice, he had to work hard to pay it back over the following ten years or so. But for him it was not work, it was almost as if he had a calling to fulfil this role.

'I have to do it,' he said. 'I don't want to do it because it can be done, I do it for the betterment of the animals. I believe animals are sentient creatures and if their lives can be improved and we have the technology and the science, we have to do it.' Noel is a man of rhetoric, passion and drama.

In fact, he had been an actor and he even has his own page on the website IMDb (Internet Movie Database). His eclectic portfolio includes an appearance in *Heartbeat* and a role in that movie classic, *The Devil's Tattoo*. Apparently he once appeared in *Casualty* and the factual show *Wildlife SOS* on the same weekend and the BBC received complaints that the latter programme included an actor pretending to be a vet!

The day of the airing of the BBC programme was a typically hot and sunny one in the Algarve. Mike and I had been the 'advance party' having arrived on the Saturday (giving us the chance to bag the best bedroom in the villa where we were staying). Mike's elderly parents were making the three-hour drive down from their home in Lisbon, whilst Mike and I were picking up his children from the airport in the afternoon. Rachael had a part-time job at a garden centre restaurant and she did not want to miss two weekends' worth of pay, so the children were coming Wednesday to Wednesday.

Whilst Rachael had flown from Jersey to Liverpool to university, it was the first time she and Chris had flown abroad without either of their parents. We were not too concerned as the journey only entailed flying from Jersey to Gatwick and then Gatwick to Faro. As they attempted to check in, Mike got a text to say that their flight had been cancelled. This was a disaster as they then had to catch another flight later that day. Frantically we called the airline and were told the children had been re-booked onto a later flight, but this meant they would not be in time to pick up the no-frills, no-changes airline flight to Portugal. Rachael and Chris were panicking at Jersey Airport and I was trying to placate them as Mike was urgently ringing round to see what alternative arrangements could be made. We had no Internet access where we were staying which only served to exacerbate the problem. We must have spent the best part of an hour and a half trying to sort out flights for the children (who at twenty and sixteen were not really children, but they were not seasoned travellers either). Finally after a bit of cajoling, the budget airline agreed to take them on a later flight for a small supplement. They would arrive much later than the mid-afternoon scheduled time. In fact, they would not be arriving till gone eight o'clock that evening.

The Bionic Vet was due to air after the ten o'clock news that night (unlike much of Europe,

Portugal is in the same time zone as the UK). We may not have had any Internet access but thankfully we did have English TV as the villa we were renting belonged to an English family.

Mike and I went to the airport, hoping the flight would be on time. Rachael had texted just before they left London and it seemed they were due to take-off on schedule. We parked the car and went into the Arrivals Hall and anxiously read the board. Phew, the plane was on time. All we hoped now was that there would be no delays in getting through customs or getting the baggage. We went upstairs to the observation deck whilst we waited. Finally we saw people from their flight arrive and queue for passport control. Most of them looked pale and tired, but no doubt they were looking forward to a holiday in the sun. We spotted Rachael and Chris towards the back of the queue.

'Hurry up!' I said out loud but of course they couldn't hear me from behind the glass partition. They hadn't even looked up and seen that Mike and I were there. We went back downstairs and about fifteen minutes later they emerged with their bags. We all hugged, relieved that after a long day for them, they had finally made it. We paid for the parking and piled their bags into the car. Thank goodness they had travelled light as our hire car was possibly the smallest one for hire in Portugal. When we had picked it up on the Saturday, the hire company had explained that the larger car we'd booked was not available until later in the week, but unfortunately, it never materialised. Some time after, we read in a local paper that because of the recession there was a chronic shortage of cars available that year, so I suppose we were lucky to get one at all.

We got back to the villa at around ten o'clock and the children greeted their grandparents whilst we poured drinks for everyone. There was no time for them to unpack or take a refreshing dip in the pool. We hardly ever watched television on holiday but today was different.

We settled down on the leather sofas, not knowing anything about the final cut. This was it.

The episode was called *Give a Cat Two New Feet—Done!* We watched as Mike arrived at Fitzpatrick Referrals with Oscar to meet Noel for the first time.

'This is going to be embarrassing!' exclaimed Mike. Like most people not used to being on television, all you notice are the things you don't like about yourself. I thought he came across really well; articulate with a lovely voice that I have always found so attractive.

The programme went on to show the operation. We were told that because the operations featured in the series were so gruesome, it had to be broadcast after the nine o'clock watershed. I could not watch as Noel drilled into Oscar's ankles. How people who did not know the outcome could have watched, I've no idea. The show also featured an eight-year-old Labrador, Mayo, who had crippling arthritis. One of his front paws had collapsed and, unless the bones could be fused together, offering him new rigid support, he would have serious problems. Noel said he was inspired by the X-Men and came up with an extraordinary surgical solution that he dubbed his 'Wolverine Technique'.

The show ended with Oscar taking his first steps after having his first set of feet attached.

He had been sedated and as he came round Noel encouraged him to walk across the consulting room floor.

Mike and I sat hand in hand as we saw him take his first few steps. He was not just walking though; he was dashing about at quite a pace as he raced to explore the outer edges of the room.

'Take it easy, take it easy,' said Noel, smiling, sitting on the floor as Oscar ran about looking for an exit. Noel blocked the doorways with big rolls of paper towels to prevent him going through but Oscar was not deterred. He tried to climb over them. 'He's trying to jump!' laughed Noel. 'He's not supposed to do that the first time he jumps.'

'That is amazing. He's come on so well since then too!' Mike said as we were all glued to the screen.

When we got home from Portugal we read a comment on a website forum that encapsulated it perfectly.

'No hobbling around confused, no weak wobbly stumbling, just "Hey, got any tuna in this joint? Nah, don't get up, I'll find it myself".'

The show ended with Noel cuddling Oscar and saying, 'He's just the best cat in the world. I can't tell you how good it feels to keep him alive,' and he kissed his head.

By now Mike and I (and we would later learn, many viewers) had tears rolling down our cheeks. Mike's parents and children were also moved; the whole clan were 'tearing up' as Chris described it.

'What a brave boy,' I said, barely able to get my words out.

On screen Noel continued: 'To think he would have been put to sleep. It could have so easily gone the other way. He was just really lucky to be in the right place at the right time and the vet that sent him knew that this was available, otherwise this magnificent life would have been snuffed out just like that.'

As the credits rolled we were beside ourselves. Oscar was a very lucky cat indeed.

CHAPTER 14

THE WEIRD AND WONDERFUL WORLD

We knew Oscar's story would make the local news as it was something different and our local paper, the *Jersey Evening Post*, has to produce a paper six days a week, to be read by the majority of the 97,000 population. Similarly, Channel Television produces a half-hour TV news show every day of the week, so they are always looking for news. They seemed to appreciate a 'feel-good factor' story such as Oscar's to break up what can otherwise be fairly miserable news, especially in times of economic recession. What took us by surprise was the sheer level of global interest in his story. Within days of the story breaking via the press release on 25 June 2010, an Internet search of 'Oscar the bionic cat' brought over seven million hits. Even over two years later, a search still returns over two million pages. When footage (no pun intended) of him walking on his new his feet was uploaded on YouTube it received over one and a half million hits. When we agreed to participate in media for Fitzpatrick Referrals, we had no idea what it would entail. We did interviews for both the BBC and ITV and as we were asked similar questions by the people who interviewed us, our confidence increased, although whether our delivery improved is not for us to say.

Of course, some of the facts were reported incorrectly. The media had reported that Mike was a bank manager in Jersey, whereas in fact he is a data centre manager in the IT department of a bank in Jersey. Much of the news surrounding Oscar reported that we were from 'New Jersey' and the story mutated into Oscar living on a farm. In fact, a couple of years later, when Discovery Channel came to Jersey to film for *Must Love Cats* for Animal Planet, the cameraman had been directed to look for 'Nolan Farm' rather than our rather modest cottage. He had even been told it had a white picket fence around the edge! We have no idea where that came from. We still have no idea who set up Oscar's Facebook page either, but he is much more popular than Mike and I combined, with some 900 'friends'.

One of the wonderful things that happened as a result of the publicity was the passer-by who found Oscar came forward. We had always wondered who she was and if we would ever find out. Her name is Francine Waters and we are forever grateful to her for going out of her way to help Oscar. Without her, he would have almost certainly died in the field.

A couple of weeks after the story broke, Peter Haworth rang us from New Era Veterinary Hospital.

'I've had a Japanese TV company on the phone wanting to run a story on Oscar.'

'OK, do they want me to call them?' asked Mike.

'Actually it's a bit of an unusual one. They want

to know if Oscar has caused any miracles,' said Peter wryly.

'The miracle is he's still alive!' laughed Mike.

'I told them that he'd had two other car accidents so he had definitely more than the usual nine lives, but they wanted to know if miracles had happened to the people he'd come into contact with!' explained Peter.

'Good grief,' said Mike, 'I'll give them a call. I'll let you know if he turns the water into wine,' he joked.

As far as we are aware, to date, Oscar has yet to perform any miracles, although we have to say, seeing him running around content with life is a miracle enough for us.

Oscar's story was taking over our lives. We received messages from friends of friends who enquired after his wellbeing and all conversations with friends and family invariably started with 'How's Oscar?'

Oscar, it seemed, was an inspiration to many people; amongst them disabled people, many of whom hoped that Oscar's treatment might become available to them. Noel had always emphasised how he would like to collaborate with the human medical world to advance this type of procedure and in fact implants were already being used on humans. On the BBC disability-related blog page entitled 'Ouch!' a contributor wrote the following on the day Oscar's story hit the news: 'This technology is being tested in humans. An interesting reversal of the usual state of affairs.'

Indeed, a year before, a British man agreed to undergo surgery to have such a device implanted. Implants have various advantages including no more pain or discomfort common to socket technology; fast, easy, accurate and repeatable attachment of prosthetic limbs and improved control of the limb. For him, being invited to trial this procedure was both exciting but also daunting. He said 'the use of the implant would mean no need for weight bearing by my soft tissue, removing the major drawback of a conventional prosthetic'. However, there was a risk that if it did not go to plan he would not be able to use any prosthetic at all. He was aware that a similar operation had been performed on an arm amputee with good results; however a leg implant is much bigger and has to take more force. Just before surgery he was advised that another patient had also received a leg implant, which reassured him.

The operation was a success but thereafter followed a lengthy rehabilitation process including intensive physiotherapy. It was some months before he was fitted with his prosthetic leg and he had to re-learn how to share the weight between his two legs. Gradually he was able to walk with sticks and ultimately without any arm support at all.

His remarkable recovery meant that in September 2010 he successfully climbed the highest mountain in Africa, Kilimanjaro, as part of a team raising funds for the Limbless Association, taking only a day longer than able-bodied people. He has continued to undertake fund-raising challenges including a 100-kilometre nocturnal cycle ride in London in the summer of 2012.

When interviewed he said, 'It just feels like they've given me my leg back. If I'd had this when I first had my amputation, you know, I would never have really felt disabled in the first place.'

One of Noel's pioneering concepts is 'One Medicine'—a fusion of technologies advancing veterinary and human medicines in tandem. If Oscar's operation, whatever the outcome, can help human patients in the future, we believe the surgery to have been worthwhile.

Oscar's story continued to capture people's imagination and this story caught our eye.

The Handicats! is a new online comic book starring Homer the Fearless Feline and his super-buddy sidekick, Ajax the Bionic Kitty. In their first adventure, Episode #1: Of Origins and Oil Spills, Homer and Ajax save the world and plug the Gulf oil spill using a bionic furball!

Homer the Fearless Feline is Gwen Cooper's cat which she took in as a three-week-old kitten. He had to have his eyes removed following a severe eye infection and she tells his story in the book *Homer's Odyssey*, a charming tale which became a *New York Times* bestseller.

Homer's mum, Gwen Cooper, explained the genesis of *The Handicats!* project:

Back in June, a news story about a 'bionic cat' in England who'd had his two hind legs replaced with artificial limbs spread throughout the online CATverse. We're long-time comic book fans in this house, and we compare the real-life Homer to the Marvel Comics superhero Daredevil, all the time. 'We should team Homer up with a bionic cat,' I said to my husband, 'and the two of them could fight crime and have adventures together.' We were amused by the idea, although we didn't plan to actually do anything with it. Then, while we were watching the July 4th fireworks, my husband had an image of two cats—one black and one white—parachuting together across a fireworks-strewn sky.

Thus, *The Handicats!* were born. It seemed appropriate to have them tackle the Gulf oil spill. As a Florida native who grew up in the waters of the Atlantic and the Gulf, I viewed the daily news stories about the disaster with horror. Watching the oil spread—destroying the communities and ecosystems and marine life that formed some of my earliest memories—was like watching my childhood disappear. It seemed like the only solution would have to involve some sort of superhuman intervention.

The drawings by Mark Martel are bright and colourful and have all the impact of a great comic strip.

Homer plays 'himself' in the comic strip whilst Oscar becomes 'Ajax' and sports three prosthetic limbs rather than two. Oscar's manifestations were appearing in all sorts of unlikely places. On a website selling shoes, one black patent pair appeared to have white stilettos in the photo and a reviewer says, 'Ugly Aldo shoes resemble Oscar the Bionic cat'. She had a point.

There is also an unofficial fan club website for Lee Majors (who played the title role of the bionic man in the *Six Million Dollar Man* TV series), called Cyborg, and they have named Oscar as their official site mascot.

I came across an accomplished American artist,

Cheri O'Brien, who had painted two gouache portraits of Oscar which are now for sale for hundreds of dollars. She told me that she had painted them as part of a series she had been commissioned to do on wounded animals. She said she had opened the newspaper where she saw the picture of Oscar and had been inspired to paint him. I bought one of the portraits for Mike for Christmas and had it shipped across the Atlantic. It was carefully packaged and wrapped in layers of bubble wrap and brown paper. I decided not to undo it all, instead wrapped the whole package in Christmas gift paper and hid it in the wardrobe until Christmas Day.

When the time came Mike was intrigued as to what the package could be as he undid the various layers. He had not seen the picture previously although I had mentioned it to him before I had made the decision to buy it. He was delighted as he exposed the picture. She had copied one of Jim Incledon's photographs and had captured his big round eyes and big face perfectly. She had situated him in an abstract field of corn, standing proudly on his new feet. What I had failed to notice when I bought the picture was that she had also painted Oscar's severed feet which were lying in blood at the bottom of the picture amidst the corn. Oh dear. It was a beautiful portrait but to my mind, spoilt by this rather gruesome representation. We have hung the picture on the wall, but it is hidden on the staircase so people only look at it in passing and hopefully don't notice the bloody feet.

The news story was everywhere from the *LA Times* to the Australian *Daily Telegraph*. It featured in the *Taipei Times*, *The Himalayan Times* and the

Jakarta Globe. In total the story was published in some eighty-five countries in print media that we know of, and even more online. In the following months we were not surprised to see his story in *Your Cat* magazine, however, we were somewhat bemused to see his picture in lads' mag *Nuts* where he appeared in a 'weird and wonderful' feature.

One amusing website wrote: 'The doctors fitted Oscar with custom-made, computer-generated prosthetic legs fused into his body. If this type of technology is available now, it's just a matter of time before cats all over the world start getting themselves fitted with stronger, more powerful limbs, and eventually entire synthetic bodies.'

This was followed by a series of photos of Oscar's head superimposed on various futuristic bodies so he became 'Terminator cat', 'Cylon Cat' and 'Voltron cat' amongst others. It was amazing how people spent their time.

The feedback on message boards, forums and blogs was overwhelmingly good. Following the broadcast of *The Bionic Vet* comments included:

'Will someone put the heart back into my chest.'

'Wonderful story. Love Oscar. Love the vet.'

'Got some dust in my eye. Damn dust.'

'Once again I am amazed at how animals simply accept things as they are . . . and I am amazed that there are still humans in this world willing to go above and beyond to help them.'

Noel himself was attracting his fair share of female admirers. The girls at my office asked if he would do a calendar. I asked Noel, but unfortunately for his many fans he declined.

One blogger asked, 'Is that vet-um-single? (hums casually)'

Of course, as to be expected, there were negative comments too. Typical of this reaction was:

'While it is nice that an individual cat didn't have to be put down, I would think it would be more animal friendly to adopt a cat from an animal shelter instead then also donate the rest of the money which was not spent on a single cat for the improvement to that animal shelter.'

And:

'Shouldn't these ground-breaking surgeries and their exorbitant cost and technological-scientific equipment be reserved for the humans? A pet doesn't know about mortality, existence or spirituality.'

Interestingly, nearly all the negatives were countered by someone with the opposite point of view. In an interview, the question of spending so much money on a pet was put to Noel and he said, 'It's not your decision what people spend money on. You can't say it's only a cat or a dog because it is not for you to judge what the relationship between the animal and the person is.'

In every interview we did and even in casual conversation, the question of cost was raised. We were perceived in some quarters to be wealthy Jersey residents living in a tax haven with endless disposable income to throw at our pets. The truth was slightly different. We were lucky to live on such a picturesque island as Jersey. Mike's father had come to the island in the 1960s from Liverpool and earned a living in all manner of ways, from running a guest house to working as a bookkeeper and a driving instructor. Mike's mother is Portuguese and came to the island to find work too. It is believed around fifteen to twenty per cent of Jersey's population is of Portuguese descent, mainly from Madeira (although Mike's mother is from Lisbon). They met when Mike's father (Mike Senior) was working as a milkman, and his mother, Cristina, was a housekeeper in a large house. Despite the fact that Cristina's English was as poor as Mike Senior's Portuguese, they fell in love, married and had Mike, who is known in the family as Little Mike. A misnomer if ever there was one, for he is a strapping six-footer. I moved to Jersey from London in 1991 to work in a hotel before I moved into financial recruitment in the late 1990s. Mike and I were very much an average family living with an average income living in an average house.

Oscar's bills were covered by insurance for the first £4,000 of his treatment. The cost of his operation, research and development of both his implants and his feet, and his rehabilitation were largely borne by people who were heavily involved in the process. No figure has been put on the actual cost but estimates vary from around £20,000 to £50,000. If we had been asked to pay this ourselves we would not have been able to proceed. We will be forever grateful for all the support we have been given, particularly from Fitzpatrick Referrals.

CHAPTER 15

Oscar and the Small Screen

In August 2010 Noel hosted what he called 'VetFest', an open day at his practice to thank primarily the referring vets and also his staff. We were invited as 'parents of Oscar' who was by now a media sensation. Oscar was still living there, some nine months after first arriving. He effectively now had a wing of the practice to himself. This comprised two huge rooms that formerly housed the physiotherapy suite, which was being rebuilt in a new area. Fortunately for Oscar this area was temporarily redundant, thus affording him plenty of space to roam and exercise. Furthermore the windows were floor to ceiling, which meant he could survey the countryside and watch the wildlife. It was nearly as good as *Springwatch*. He was much loved by the staff and had a constant stream of visitors giving him love and affection. He could never have too much of that.

Noel had also formed a strong bond with his long-term resident. He said he would go and sit with Oscar when he was working on academic papers, often being inspired by Oscar's contribution to his career. Oscar had a lot to thank Noel for and he responded by being the cuddliest, gentlest cat there was.

We were not sure what to expect at VetFest. We did know there were going to be musical tribute bands and a performance by 'The Saw Doctors' who it transpired were Noel's favourite band. We knew that there was going be a hog roast and an appearance by Chris Evans, whose dog had been treated by Noel. Above all we knew we were going to see Oscar for the first time in several months.

As soon as we arrived at Fitzpatrick Referrals we were introduced to the people from the PR company who had been responsible for Oscar's media presence. To our total surprise we were to be filmed for *Sixty Minutes,* an Australian TV show that focused on news stories. The production team of five had flown over specifically to film the story of Oscar and the implant surgery and this included an interview with us, which we rather hastily scheduled to take place at twelve noon the next day.

'His story is fantastic,' said one of the PR girls.

'We were ridiculously busy the day the story broke!' she explained.

'We couldn't believe it either!' we said.

Noel greeted us with heartfelt hugs as he prepared for the long day ahead. Well, eleven in the morning to midnight probably was not a long day for him, but it seemed that it was going to be for us.

As we walked around the timbered building to the large marquee where the main event was to be held, we saw that Oscar's temporary residence, the old physiotherapy suite, was being used as a space for exhibitors at the event.

'I'm afraid we've had to put Oscar back in one of the kennels for today. I'll get him down for you,' explained Noel.

Amidst all the commotion, we went to see him in one of the consulting rooms. There was little doubt he recognised us—he let out a little meow and trotted over to us as Noel put him down on the floor.

'Hello boy,' said Mike to Oscar as the little black fur ball headbutted him, looking for affection. He walked around the room having a good sniff as he went. His gait had improved a great deal since we had last seen him a couple of months previously and he was wearing new feet, which were even more blade-like in design. The idea was that they would be more comfortable for him to emulate normal walking. They had been made of resin with a metal brace that screwed onto the exposed part of the implant. The soles of the feet were made from human shoes—'Crocs' in fact. Mike and I never thought anyone in our household would be seen dead in Crocs, but then Oscar was never one for falling in with the crowd.

Whilst we fussed over Oscar and fed him meaty stick treats, the music of the Amy Winehouse tribute act that was playing on stage could be heard in the distance. Closer to where we were, we could hear a cacophony of people's voices and dogs barking as guests were given guided tours around the facilities. Amongst the guests were various people whose animals had appeared on the recently aired *The Bionic Vet* and it was great to see so many of the pets had made a remarkable recovery. Little did people know that, arguably, the biggest star of the show was actually there at the practice that day. We were very glad that Noel's overriding view was that Oscar should be kept out of sight and away from the noisy throngs of people.

We spent over an hour with Oscar, sitting on the floor stroking him as he padded around with two quiet front paws and two clickety back feet, sounding like a woman walking about in her stilettos. When he finally settled down to go to sleep we fetched the nurse to take him back to his kennel.

The aroma of the hog roast lured us back to the main party tent, which was by now filled with a couple of hundred people. The evening rumbled on with Noel, accompanied by broadcaster Chris Evans, giving out awards to his staff in recognition of their commitment. We imagined that people working for Noel would be inspired but tired! Alistair McGowan, who we had been introduced to earlier, came on stage and did a superb set including impressions of not only media and sports stars, but also of Noel himself. He mimicked his dramatic persona and Irish accent perfectly.

We topped up our wine and were getting into the music of The Saw Doctors, when Lizzie, one of the PR girls, came up to us.

'I'm off now, but I just wanted to check you're OK to be back here tomorrow morning at 11 a.m.?' she asked.

'We thought it was twelve noon, lucky you said something!' I replied.

'*Sixty Minutes* is at twelve noon, but NBC is at eleven o'clock,' she clarified.

'NBC! We didn't know about that one!' Mike replied. She went on to advise us, rather belatedly, that we were going to do a live video link-up to *Today*, America's biggest breakfast show. We did know that NBC were interested in the story as they had called us to see if we would agree to be filmed, but we did not appreciate it was going to be a live broadcast. Thank goodness I had packed my curling tongs.

The next morning I got up extra early, a) to take some painkillers and a litre of water as I tried to dilute the stirrings of a hangover and b) to apply all the necessary make-up associated with being on television.

'I think it's actually Oscar they're interested in filming,' Mike said to me in a curiously convincing Australian accent with a rising tag at the end.

'I know, I know, but you don't know who might be watching!' I joked.

As we headed down the country lane to Fitzpatrick Referrals my heart sank.

'Oh my gosh! Look!' I exclaimed as I took in the sight of the NBC van with the gigantic satellite dish on its roof.

I was not quite sure if we were ready for live broadcasting. After brief introductions with the crew we were wired up with microphones and shown to a trestle table which had been placed in the empty car park, where we would be filmed.

'If you have Oscar standing on the table in front of you, Jenna, the anchor, will interview you. We've got about twenty minutes till we air,' said the producer. The team rigged up lights and tested the sound quality and the link to New York.

We just needed Noel, who was nowhere to been seen, and, of course, Oscar. Another ten minutes passed and there was still no sign of either of them. Where were they? Well, we knew where Oscar was, but we did not know how to go about getting him as being Sunday the practice was technically shut. Time ticked on. No sign.

'You can't film out here!' Noel emerged from one of the side doors of the building, slightly stubbly but all the more handsome for it. 'Oscar's an indoor cat now. He's not allowed out here!' he said.

'Surely he'll be OK on the table if the owners hold him. It'll only be for ten minutes,' replied the cameraman reasonably.

'Sorry guys, we've got to go inside,' answered an unyielding Noel. It was clear to everyone that there were to be no compromises.

Mike and I felt like helpless bystanders as frantic calls were made to New York to see if we could have a later slot, whilst the crew hurriedly reeled in light cables, moved the lighting stands and followed Noel to the indoor venue.

A few minutes later we were in Oscar's makeshift home of the physiotherapy wing. After his day in the kennels he was back 'home'. As the sound and cameraman took their positions and adjusted the lighting, Oscar took it all in his stride. He was happily lying by Mike and me as we sat on the floor waiting for the interview. He was fazed by nothing.

It went seamlessly, Mike and I instinctively knew who should speak next and although we could not see the American anchor, we heard her and talked straight to camera. Oscar sat compliantly by our legs. It was all over in a matter of minutes. The crew packed up and departed whilst we prepared for our next interview with the crew for *Sixty Minutes*.

Oscar was by now getting used to having cameras pointed at him and was far more chilled about the whole experience than his parents were. He was not a demanding star, although if you wanted to see him walk or run about on his new feet, then tuna had to be available at all times.

Noel duly produced a bowl and Oscar did everything that was required of him footage-wise for the Australian *Sixty Minutes* show. This weekly current affairs programme runs four fifteen-minute features per week and this slot was focusing on bionic implants in humans and animals. Liam Bartlett, the handsome anchor, put us at ease as he ran through the formula. Oscar wandered around happily, intrigued by more new people and once he'd had enough attention for the day, went and sat on his rug in the corner of the room.

Liam asked questions about the accident itself and the decision-making process we went through. Once again we emphasised that we only agreed to go ahead with it on the understanding that Oscar would have a good quality of life, and not just because we didn't want to lose a pet.

Towards the end of the interview Liam concluded, 'As for Oscar the bionic cat, he's been living at the practice since his accident last October. And when he does go home, there'll be no more frolicking in the field for him.'

Mike quipped, 'We've grounded him effectively, because the last time we let him out, he came back legless.'

CHAPTER 16

MOVING ON AND SAYING GOODBYE

Back at home life continued as normal, the house renovation eating up most of our time and money. We watched programmes like *Grand Designs* and marvelled at how people managed to convert a derelict water mill to a glass-fronted, eco-friendly six-bedroom house with its own recycling plant and landscaped garden in six months, whilst it had taken us over three years to get as far as we had. We were, however, now at the fun bit of planning a new kitchen and bathroom. We shopped around and plumped for a country-style cream kitchen with state-of-the-art appliances so I could continue to indulge my love of cooking. The bathroom, although small, was going to be like a boutique hotel with travertine (limestone) tiles from floor to ceiling, a circular bowl-type washbasin and bath with a drench shower. I could not wait.

'You should try to sell your old basin and toilet,' the builder said, looking at the ornate, shell-shaped basin painted with roses complete with matching loo. I looked into this, and as I thought, they were at the height of being out of fashion, so they ended up being dumped with the old kitchen.

Our next-door neighbour, Jim, a portly man in his seventies, came round to look at the work in progress. Over the years he had seen successive owners make alterations to the property, but conceded that the people from whom we had bought the house had done very little in their ten years of residence, hence the state of disrepair.

'I couldn't wait to see the back of that dreadful old kitchen,' I said as I waved goodbye to the white Formica units with pale blue handles that were being thrown into the skip.

'I fitted those twenty-eight years ago,' admitted ex-builder Jim.

Back pedalling, I replied, 'Well it was built to last and it certainly did its time.'

As the house started to change significantly inside Mike remarked, 'Oscar won't recognise the place.'

And herein lay the problem. Would Oscar ever be returning to us? It seemed very unlikely. The updates we had from Fitzpatrick Referrals were less frequent which we just put down to 'no news is good news'. We assumed he was progressing well and looked forward to hearing more when there was more to say.

Shortly after we returned home from VetFest,

Noel advised us that Oscar could not remain at the practice indefinitely, which of course we knew. Matters were expedited when work got underway for the development of the new physiotherapy wing, effectively rendering Oscar homeless. Mike and I were torn about what to do for the best.

Part of us felt that we had done so much for Oscar, but he did not feel like our pet any more. He was in Noel's very safe custody but it was not the ending we had anticipated when we set out on this journey. When we entered the process we did it on the proviso that Oscar would be able to enjoy a similar life to the one he had before and it was important to us that this meant being an outdoor cat. Peter from New Era was also under the impression that he would be able to be an outdoor cat. Noel, however, pointed out that it would just be too dangerous for him. Whilst we do not have foxes in Jersey, his ability to get away from traffic (which, to be fair, was never a strong point of his) would be impeded and furthermore, if his feet got entangled in brambles and suchlike he might not be able to escape. It made perfect sense that he should be an indoor cat, but at the same time, it was not exactly what we had hoped for.

Many people have suggested to us that if the cats were indoor cats, then Oscar would not have suffered his terrible fate. That is true and you cannot argue with that fact, but at the same time, we wanted our cats to have enriched lives and the ability to hunt, roam and enjoy the sensory experiences that only the outside world could give them. We were well aware that keeping cats inside was safer in that there was no traffic, no parasites such as fleas or ticks and no contact with other cats, therefore giving protection against Feline Immunodeficiency Virus (FIV) and Feline Leukaemia. They would also not get lost or stumble across poisons. Despite this, like most British cat owners, we did not want to restrict such a free-spirited animal as a cat, and therefore it was not even a conscious decision, more of a rite of passage, allowing Oscar and Poppy to go outside. If we had more cats in the future, would we still allow them to go outside after everything that has happened to Oscar?

The argument for having indoor cats is certainly gathering momentum and often people's personal experiences change their viewpoint. In her article entitled 'Should Cats be allowed Outdoors Without Supervision?', American cat lover Franny Syufy revisited a previous argument she had written, advocating that cats had the right to enjoy the freedom of being allowed out. However, when her beloved cat, Shannon, was diagnosed with FIV and died a year later, she recognised that had she not allowed her cat out when he was young, he would never have contracted the disease and died. In her article she describes how her older outdoor cat becomes depressed and miserable if he is confined, whereas her younger cats, having been indoor cats all their lives (with a supervised area of contained garden), are well adjusted to being inside. Supporters of indoor cats argue that it is possible to provide just as stimulating an environment inside, with climbing frames, scratching posts, indoor grass and toys, so the cats are in no way hard done by. It is probably a myth that outdoor cats spend all their 'outside time' hunting and climbing. The truth of the matter is they are more likely to be curled up napping in the sun, as Oscar found out to his cost.

Despite this strong argument, we stand by our decision to allow our cats to have the right to roam and should we acquire more cats in the future, they too will be outdoor cats.

On the other hand, if we did bring Oscar home, we were concerned about how we could cope with him practically. Our downstairs area comprises a lounge/dining room leading on to a small enclosed garden and a kitchen and a hallway with a door and cat flap leading to a rear courtyard. Buzz, Lou and Poppy came and went as they chose and roamed around the house at will. Buzz and Lou both slept (most of the day) in the lounge. Oscar would have to be shut in the lounge all day whilst we were at work and the others would be shut out of it. Furthermore, in his rooms at Fitzpatrick Referrals, he could sit by the French windows and gaze at the fields in the Surrey countryside. Our lounge would only afford him a view of a few flower beds. Also, how would Oscar feel living with other cats that could come and go when he couldn't? It did not seem fair.

'If we win the lottery we can move and get a house with a big conservatory so he can look out but still have space to roam,' mused Mike. Until that happened we had to accept our position and it was around this time that a new phrase entered our daily lives: 'It is what it is.'

People regularly asked us how Oscar was doing and they too wondered when he was coming home. It was almost embarrassing saying we did not know. In late summer Noel asked us for a decision. He made it clear to us that Oscar was our cat and the decision lay with us, but at the same time, he would be happier if Oscar was close by as he could then regularly check up on him, change his feet as necessary and generally keep an eye on him.

We were torn, could we really give up on the little fellow now? Noel had offered to get him rehomed with one of his staff. The advantages of that were plain to see: he would have the best medical care right on his doorstep and would not have to make the long journey overseas to get home. He would, we presumed, be living in a more spacious environment than we could provide.

We talked and talked about what would be best. We spoke to Peter who said he could continue with Oscar's care from Jersey and he could liaise with Noel as to any on-going treatment.

'I really want the boy back,' said Mike as we weighed up the pros and cons.

'I do too, but I don't think he'd have such a good life here, trapped in the lounge all day.'

'We might move one day and once he's rehomed we may never have the opportunity get him back. If he's settled somewhere else, it wouldn't be fair to take him away,' replied Mike.

'I only want what's best for him,' I said.

'Me too.'

We talked and talked forever, going round in circles, neither of us willing to make the ultimate decision with regards to his fate. In my heart I thought he would be better off close to Noel in England. I knew this would break Mike's heart. Unfortunately, we did not have family close to Surrey that would be able to mind Oscar for us. We had friends there who did offer to look after him but they had another outdoor cat, so we had to rule that out for the same reasons we thought we could not bring him home. I had never heard of a household that had a mix of indoor and outdoor cats. For one crazy moment Mike and I even talked about moving to England ourselves, but work and family commitments in Jersey pretty soon ruled that notion out.

Noel needed a decision so we reluctantly agreed that he should have Oscar re-housed near him. He was going to move in with Matt Connor, the project manager at Fitzpatrick Referrals. We had met Matt briefly at VetFest and we learned from Noel that he lived by himself but had children who visited him regularly.

'He's got a lovely house in the country,' Noel told us. 'It's got lots of windows for Oscar to look through, so he'll be absolutely grand there. He'll be far better off in a family house than here. You can come and see him whenever you want.'

We thanked Noel for everything he had done and with a mixture of happiness that Oscar, who had spent almost half his life in medical practices, was finally going home and disappointment that it was not our home. We wished him well.

*   *   *

Back at home a few months later, all was not well with Buzz. Ever since I had known her she did not like being picked up, but occasionally it was necessary to move her from one seat to another, if we wanted to sit down, for example. She was reluctant to move too far if we had visitors because she was very interested in human conversations. She also liked a party and loud music did not bother her at all. I could imagine her telling Poppy, 'Back

172

in the day, I was real raver.' Buzz was now fifteen years of age, and apart from a couple of bouts of vomiting, had enjoyed a healthy life. She was not a particularly big cat but if she had been a human she may well have had a tummy tuck as her flab did hang dangerously close to the floor. Her very dense fur, however, masked the fact that Buzz was shrinking.

One evening, as she lay obstructing access to the cupboard that housed the ironing board ('Sorry, Mike, I couldn't iron your shirts as Buzz was in the way'), I picked her up and was shocked. She weighed next to nothing. It was as if she was hollow underneath her furry coat. I took upstairs and put her on the scales. She weighed 2.8 kilograms. A normal range for a British Shorthair is 5–7 kilograms.

The next morning we took her to New Era Veterinary Hospital. Buzz was found to have a significant mass in her stomach area and the vet gave us three options: they could undertake exploratory surgery to see if it could be removed, they could give her some medication including antibiotics which could prolong her life, or we could take her home and let nature take its course. We went for the second option, which to our relief is what the vet said she would have done too, but she was obliged to give us the choices.

Buzz seemed comfortable and was still eating, but she was also drinking a great deal more than usual. She had been lapping the water from my bedside glass for a few weeks now and I had found it rather endearing. I should have known it was a sign that all was not well.

One day I got home from work to find Buzz, who

rarely ventured outside except to do her ablutions, sitting on a pile of leaves in the garden. It was a very cold day, even for November, so I picked her up and brought her inside. She did not settle and pushed herself through the cat flap back in to the cooling night air. I did not feel comfortable about it.

'They go away to die,' I said to Mike.

'Maybe she's just got a fever and is really hot,' he answered. Nonetheless, we set up a litter tray in the lounge (we had them in various sizes and styles thanks to Oscar's numerous periods of convalescence). We placed a bowl of water and some fresh fish in there too, much to lazy Lou's delight, who was most put out when she found out it was not room service for her. We brought Buzz in and shut the lounge door as we sat with her and watched her move from place to place. She did not seem distressed, more resigned and unsettled.

She was not interested in the food or even the water. I put some water on my fingers—she had always been an over-zealous licker. Now when I was encouraging it, she was not interested. She went to the litter tray but instead of using it, she just slumped down in it. It was heartbreaking to watch her.

'I think we'll have to take her back down to the vet tomorrow if she's like this,' I said to Mike, as we watched the most sociable of our pets looking increasingly miserable. At one point she tried to jump onto the sofa but she somehow misjudged it and fell awkwardly back on to the floor. Her legs seemed to be losing their strength. Periodically she would curl up as if to go to sleep, only to get up a few minutes later. She was clearly uncomfortable.

I went up to bed about eleven o'clock by which time Buzz had gone behind the television, a place she never usually visited. It was as if she was looking for somewhere private to hide. I was just settling down to sleep when Mike called me down.

'She's just made a really weird sound,' he said. Buzz was still behind the television, half standing, and half sitting. I grabbed a towel from the sofa (we had put it there earlier, trying to make her comfortable) and picked her up and cuddled her. She went straightaway. Her body went into a spasm and then relaxed. There was no doubt what had happened.

'Goodbye, Buzz,' I said and I closed her eyes with my fingers like they do in the movies. I wrapped the towel around her so just her little face peeped through. She really did look peaceful. Mike put his arm around my shoulder.

'We loved Buzz,' he said. I felt the tears fall down my face and I clung on to her. Lou was also in the room, but whether she could tell what had happened was hard to know as she curled up and went to sleep. Poppy was definitely oblivious to events as she bounded in demanding her nightcap of cat milk.

I had always joked that when Buzz died I was going to groom her coat properly once and for all. Funnily enough, at the time of her death her coat was probably in the best condition it had ever been.

We called the vet to arrange to take Buzz there for cremation. We wanted to take her there and then rather than wait for the morning. I wasn't keen to witness rigor mortis setting in. I held her in my arms, still wrapped in the towel, as we drove down to New Era. The nurse greeted us with sympathy and kindness and we went through to the consulting room where we gently laid Buzz on the examination table. We said a last goodbye and drove home in silence. It was the only out-of-hours trip to the vet's that we had ever made that did not involve Oscar.

Returning back, the house seemed empty with just two cats.

CHAPTER 17

LETTING GO

Over the following weeks there was a significant change in Buzz's sister, Lou. She was not deteriorating in the way Buzz had been in her last few weeks; on the contrary, she suddenly got a new spring in her paws. She started going outside more, even though winter was proving to be a cold one. Her fur became glossier and her eyes, which for many years had been prone to weeping, became brighter. She was eating well and just seemed generally happier.

It did not take us too long to realise that she was the one person/cat in the household who did not mourn Buzz's passing. In fact, she positively relished it. For the first time in her life she could walk from room to room without being hissed at and periodically attacked. She could choose exactly where she slept, even in Buzz's coveted spot on our bed if she so desired. She could eat her entire meal without Buzz nudging her out of the way. She was delighted that her sister had buzzed off.

Now, with fewer cats in the household, the

dynamics altered again. Poppy did not take long to assume Buzz's mantle of Alpha Cat, a role she had been preparing for under Buzz's tutelage for two years, whilst Lou stayed at the bottom of the heap. Lou did not mind at all. She was happy now bully Buzz was not around.

Seeing Lou become so much more relaxed and happy made our grieving at the loss of Buzz much easier to bear. Whilst we missed the friendly, sociable old girl, Lou was clearly pleased that her cantankerous, bad-breathed sister had gone, enabling her to finally come out of her shell.

Our house seemed very quiet, especially as Poppy only popped in for meals and Lou was asleep most of the time.

'I really want a ginger kitten,' I whined like a child. I fancied a big ginger tomcat that would sit on my lap and display characteristics more akin to the cats of children's literature.

Mike, however, was more practical on the matter. 'That road outside gets too busy. I think we should wait until we move.'

It was true; although Oscar's 'other' accidents had not happened at peak times, it was still a relatively fast road. The speed limit in Jersey is 40 miles an hour and this road, being straight, tempted drivers to frequently exceed that. Even sticking to the speed limit was no guarantee that a cat would not be hit.

At Christmas in 2010 we had our annual staff lunch at a restaurant called Danny's in the picturesque fishing village of St Aubin. The menu at Danny's was often quirky, with mouth-watering offerings simply entitled 'Skippy', 'Moo', 'Quack' and suchlike. Their name belied the complex dishes, for example 'Shell' is 'Pan-fried Jersey hand-dived scallops with ceviche salsa, bean and rocket salad' and 'Porky' is 'Pork fillet on crushed [Jersey] royals, green beans with a wild mushroom and grain mustard cream, and parsnip chips'. Settling down in the crowded conservatory, trying to make ourselves heard over the noisy table next to us (which, it transpired, was the tax office— it must have been the relief of being allowed to have fun) we ordered our festive fayre. I looked around and was suddenly taken aback. Sitting on the other side of the glass door was a familiar, big, fat ginger cat asking to be let in. A waiter obliged and, with his tail in the air, the cat walked boldly round the restaurant seemingly looking in vain for an empty chair. Out of luck, he settled against a wall, completely unfazed by fifty people having their annual knees-up, frenetic waiting staff rushing about with arms full of plates and the sound of Slade coming through the music system.

'Excuse me,' I asked, attracting the attention of a stressed-out waiter, 'what's that cat called?'

I knew it. It was Moss who had lived next door to me when I had the flat. His sociable nature could reach new dizzy heights now.

*   *   *

We kept in touch with Noel to find out how Oscar was getting on. He was continuing to do well by all accounts and was enjoying living in Matt's house. We missed him dreadfully but took comfort in the fact that he was thriving.

'When are you going to bring him back?' people frequently asked us. The truth was I thought we never would. Mike was more optimistic and held on to the belief that if we moved house then we could bring him back. As the property market continued to slump in one of the worst recessions in years, it did not seem a viable option for us.

We were conscious that a lack of physical contact with Oscar might mean that he would forget us. Some people may consider that to be a good thing, so he could continue his life happily with his new guardian. We were keen to keep in contact with him, not least to see his development.

In July 2011 we arranged to visit Oscar. Matt said he would take him to Fitzpatrick Referrals and he could have a check-up with Noel at the same time. It had been some months since we had last seen him and our first proper meeting with Matt since he took custody of him.

We were escorted to one of the familiar consulting rooms whilst we awaited Oscar and his entourage to come through the door on the other side of the room. Noel appeared first and greeted us like long-lost friends. It was really good to see him.

'Let's get Oscar and his new daddy,' Noel said. His words cut right through me. This was never the plan, but it was the reality. I knew Mike sensed it too.

Matt, a tall rangy man, came in with Oscar in his arms.

'Hey guys, great to see you. Here's the little fella!' he said putting Oscar down on the floor.

Little? I thought, looking at how Oscar had filled out. He seemed to have grown in every direction. He was big and sturdy and his black fur was dense and shiny.

'He looks massive!' I exclaimed, taken aback with this muscular cat in front of me.

Oscar came up to my hand and nuzzled me. He flicked his wonky tail and walked towards Mike, rubbing himself around his legs.

'He definitely recognises you,' Matt said.

'Do you think?' I asked.

'Yes, he's normally shy with people he's not familiar with, but he was straight over to you two.'

Oscar continued to circle round us both as Matt updated us on his progress.

'He's on a diet at the moment,' he explained. 'He suddenly started to a get a bit fat and we couldn't understand why, until one night I caught him catching a mouse that was coming in through a hole in the wall! He had obviously found a source of late night snacks.'

I was really pleased that Oscar was still able to exhibit this sort of natural behaviour.

'He's a great cat,' continued Matt, 'the only problem with him is he is totally nocturnal. Every night he jumps on the bed to headbutt me for attention, or he runs round the house with his toys and I've got wooden floors so you hear the "click click" of his back feet all over the place!'

We were delighted to see that he was in such great condition. Matt made another revelation.

'I've been letting him sit out in the garden. Not for very long and only while I'm there. He likes to have a bit of a sniff around the place.'

I wondered if Noel knew about this, remembering how he was not even allowed to sit outside on the table when we did the filming for NBC.

'I must admit, though, I thought I'd lost him the

other week. Somehow he managed to get outside without me realising, so I went out in the garden to look for him and I couldn't find him. I searched all round the house but he wasn't anywhere,' Matt went on.

If Oscar were not wandering round by my feet I would have wondered where this story was leading.

'I called him . . . but nothing. I was freaking out by now. I went round the garden to see if there was any way he could have escaped and there he was curled up asleep by the French doors! You wouldn't believe how relieved I was!'

Oh yes, we would, we said.

Matt, meanwhile, seemed like an excellent carer for Oscar. He worked closely on the design of his feet and his engineering background enabled him to modify them each time they were replaced. He spent hours studying Oscar's gait and his general mobility to assess their functionality. We left that day really happy that Oscar was in such good hands—not that we ever doubted that, but spending time with Matt made us realise that although the decision to rehouse Oscar was partly out of our hands, it had been an excellent one.

CHAPTER 18

THE DAY WE THOUGHT WE'D NEVER SEE

We left Oscar, Matt and Noel, feeling really good. We were pleased that Matt thought Oscar still recognised us. This was total vanity on our part but it did make us feel better. We were also delighted that Noel and Matt continued to love Oscar as much as we did, but best of all, Oscar seemed so well. We laughed at the poor boy having to go on a diet; he loved his food so much. A lot like us really.

Matt had also shown us pictures of his house so we could see how Oscar had spectacular views of endless fields from the floor to ceiling windows. All in all, for the time being, we could not imagine a better place for him to be.

Less than a month later, we received some news that would change everything. Matt had been renting his house and his landlord had decided he was not happy with Matt keeping pets. Initially the landlord had agreed to Oscar being there (after some negotiation), but now, for whatever reason, it seemed he was reneging on the deal. Oscar needed a new home. Noel contacted us to advise that he could look at getting Oscar rehomed if we would like him to. Our thoughts turned back to a conversation we had had with Matt when we met him the previous month.

'The main reason we can't have him home is because of the other two cats,' I had said. 'I don't know how he'd be able to understand how the other cats can come and go as they please and he would be stuck inside.'

'Cats don't think like that,' said Matt. 'Cats and dogs are intelligent in different ways and cats aren't cognisant like humans. They wouldn't compare their behaviour with other cats. They are only self-interested. I don't think they experience things like envy, so I don't think that would be a problem.'

I found Matt's take on it very interesting, although at the time thought of it as only a hypothetical scenario.

182

Mike and I were thinking the same thing.

'Do you think we should see if we can get him home?' Mike said to me.

'Wouldn't that be amazing?'

We ran through the practicalities. We already had a microchip cat flap as we had had a steady stream of tomcats coming in to the house and spraying. Word had got round about how good the food was at our house. Poppy had been microchipped as a kitten and when we took Lou to the vet's for hers, they had to double-check that we really wanted a fifteen-year-old cat chipped. The problem was solved literally overnight. We had no more unwanted visitors.

Mike explained we would have to get a second cat flap fitted, but facing the other way. Lou and Poppy would be programmed to come in through one of them and out through the other, whereas Oscar could be programmed so he could come in if he inadvertently got out, but he would not be able to go out from inside, as the flaps could be manually locked to respond to the cats' microchips.

I had no idea how we would train Lou and Poppy to use one door for coming in and the other for going out. It would mean we wouldn't have to confine Oscar to the lounge and not allow the others into it whilst we were at work. It meant life could carry on as before for Lou and Poppy but we would have the assurance that Oscar could not get out. It sounded complicated, but Mike assured me it was a possible solution.

Noel was keen to ensure that we would be happy to cope with Oscar and his special needs. He also liaised with Peter Haworth so he was up to speed with his on-going care. Within a few days of us confirming that we wanted to have him home, the wheels were in motion.

Mike boarded the ferry to England to finally bring Oscar home and met Matt at Fitzpatrick Referrals for an emotional handover. Mike packed the car with Oscar's belongings: three different sized scratching posts, a sheepskin cat bed ('He loves it,' said Matt), a play tunnel, countless squeaky and non-squeaky mice and a huge sack of his 'obesity management' food. Mike and Matt hugged each other over their shared love of a brave black cat as they said goodbye.

'I'm on my way to Poole now, but the traffic is terrible,' reported Mike when he called me on the hands-free phone from the car about half an hour into his journey.

'The satnav says I'm due to arrive at 4.10 p.m. and the boat leaves ten minutes later.'

'What will you do if you miss the boat?' I was panicking. It was a Saturday in August and the thought of Mike having to find a hotel where you could also take a cat filled me with dread. We had no friends or family in that part of the country. Furthermore, I knew that the ferries back to Jersey on the Sunday were fully booked as the original plan had been to collect Oscar on the Sunday and we had had to scrap that plan for this very reason.

'It is what it is,' replied Mike who, as usual, was completely calm when matters were out of his control.

'I'll call you later, when I know what's what,' he said as he continued on his journey.

I paced the floor, I googled hotels that would take pets, I checked whether the ferries took standby passengers. As usual, I was worrying unnecessarily as Mike rang me to say that, in the nick of time, they had made it to the ferry. Oscar had to stay in his cat carrier in the car for the three-hour journey, but at least they did not have to check in to a hotel for the night.

Some ten hours after setting off from Fitzpatrick Referrals, almost two years since his accident, Oscar was home.

We let Oscar out in the lounge, wondering if he would recognise it. He warily sniffed around the room, unsure of his bearings. Lou was asleep on the sofa; Oscar rubbed against it, his long tail tickling her face. She opened one eye, looked at him as if to say 'Oh, you're back then,' and promptly closed her eye and went back to sleep.

Poppy, his twin, was less than impressed however, when she came in to see a black cat of unknown origin in her house.

'Hi sis! I'm home. Look, I've got new feet!' he seemed to be saying as he eagerly sniffed her.

'Get off me, you imbecile!' she seemed to hiss back at him and stormed out through the cat flap in a rage.

I had spent the day clearing the floor of obstacles. One of my pet hates is the amount of wires that are in the house, although I am a fan of technology. With Mike working in IT and his son Chris studying IT at college, and with the rooms filled with an assortment of computers, TVs, phone chargers, BlackBerry chargers, DVD players, a PlayStation, satnavs, CD players and so on, there were tangles of wires everywhere. We probably could have opened a wire shop with the amount of stock we had. Why did we need so many? I had tried and failed to edit the wire population, as it

185

was really Mike's domain, but now I had a really good reason for de-wiring. We needed to make the house safe for Oscar. Between us, Mike and I had put all the unused wires in two large carrier bags under the stairs (where I was convinced they would remain for eternity). All essential wiring was neatly placed behind the relevant machine or appliance. The floors looked tidy for the first time in years. The only two places where there was still a preponderance of wires were behind the TV and the computer.

Needless to say, these were the two places that Oscar was most interested in exploring. Maybe all the males in the house had the same leanings. Within five minutes of him being home he was behind the television.

'His feet, his feet will get tangled!' I screeched.

'Come out Oscar,' I pleaded, as he sniffed the corner of the lounge. Because of the size of the TV and way it was angled in the corner, we couldn't reach over and lift him out. I couldn't believe that he was in the most hazardous place in the house so soon after his arrival.

I was astonished, though, that Oscar nimbly climbed through the wires without the slightest incident. If you did not know any better you would easily think he had sensation in his feet. He was moving around in a totally normal fashion. He lifted his back legs to just the right height when he clambered over the wires. Mike and I watched in wonder as he negotiated the hazardous tangle perfectly. It was a hollow victory, though, as I knew the incentive to clear all the wires away had disappeared in an instant.

Oscar wandered through the lounge and into

the hall and then ran up the stairs at great speed, something that took us by surprise. He could certainly run. We followed him upstairs to make sure he remained safe. Matt told us he could jump as high as a bed and jump down from any height as cats use their front paws to land. He took little time in jumping onto our bed where he soon settled down after his long journey. After a short snooze, he was up again, exploring around the house, sniffing out the food in the kitchen and familiarising himself with the enormous new litter box we had bought him. This one even had a roof to ensure maximum privacy.

It was after he had been back for a couple of days when I noticed he seemed to be hopping on three legs. To my great alarm one of his feet had fallen off. Noel had liaised with Peter about changing his feet (they would have to be changed periodically because of wear and tear), but we did not think his feet would actually detach from the implant without intervention.

'I'll just screw it on again,' said Mike as I was prepared to call the Emergency Services. Having located an appropriately-sized Phillips screwdriver, I held Oscar in my arms as Mike reattached the foot without drama. Oscar was walking around properly in no time. I dreaded the day I would have to do that. I was worried I would screw it too tight and break his leg and the thought filled me with horror.

Word soon got out that Oscar was back in town and there followed a round of TV and newspaper appearances. The story was once again in the *Jersey Evening Post,* complete with full colour picture, on the six o'clock news, and on the website of the local radio station. Everyone was delighted Oscar had returned and no one more so than us.

We had also arranged for Oscar to spend a day at New Era Veterinary Hospital. This was partly so that Peter could give him a good check-up and familiarise himself with the implants, and partly so all the nurses and other people who had looked after him so well could see how he had turned out. I must admit, Oscar did not seem too delighted when we fetched his cat carrier to transport him. He must have wondered where his next journey was going to take him. He need not have worried this time and he received a royal welcome from the team at New Era as they fussed and stroked him. When we collected him at the end of the day, we asked if he had had any food as we were mindful of his diet.

'He's had some prawns, some fish and some chicken. I don't think he had any biscuits though,' said Peter as we laughed at the one constant with Oscar: his love of a good meal.

'One thing I've noticed,' said Peter 'is his front tooth is broken and I'm going to have to take it out. We can't risk him getting an abscess or any infection which could travel down to his legs.'

We had no idea how long his tooth had been broken for. We had definitely noticed when we had seen him in England but we weren't sure if it had happened at the time of the combine harvester accident or at another time.

So poor old Oscar was booked in for yet another operation to remove his right fang. We all agreed not to do it immediately, allowing him time to settle back home for a few weeks first. We were also nervous about him having it done, simply because it entailed yet another general anaesthetic and after so many we did not know how his body would react. Despite our misgivings it went well and he came home later the same day. He was irritated by the stitches for a few days and kept shaking his head, clearly hoping they would fall out of his mouth, but he soon recovered and we hoped we could finally put the operating theatre behind him.

The tally of his missing parts was now testicles, penis, part of tail, back feet and front tooth. His artificial parts were a hip toggle, two implants and two prosthetic feet. He was certainly not the cat he used to be body-wise but personality-wise he was exactly the same as ever.

As the media frenzy died down, Oscar settled into his routine. He would sleep most of the day. Of course he favoured the human beds—he had never once set foot inside his sheepskin bed from Matt's since he had come home—in fact, we consigned it to the loft with all the other beds. If we ever get round to emptying the loft we'll take them to the Animal Shelter, they're no use to us. Oscar would get up for a bite to eat when we got home from work. He loved to play with his little squeaky mice, but hoggies remained his favourites, and they were still readily available at New Era and the pet shop. He gripped them in his front paws and used his new feet to kick them. He was using his back feet in exactly the same manner he always had done.

Oscar settled into a pretty normal life, much like the one he had led before the accident—with one main exception. He could not roam at will. We had wondered if Matt had been right and whether Oscar would not feel agitated with the other cats coming in and out as they wished. He certainly didn't seem to be. He did not try to get through the cat flap, although it was so sad when we got home from work or from an evening out to see two huge green eyes staring through the Perspex window, as he looked out onto a world that was no longer his.

We let him out into our tiny front garden where he loved sniffing the air. He was fascinated by a particular place at the bottom of the fence where he would sit for hours, lying in wait. What for, we had no idea as we had never seen any movement there. Whenever we let him outside it was the first place he raced to. Sometimes he would sit down there and his tail would sweep from side to side like a lion's. Sometimes he would click his teeth together. We didn't know what was catching his attention. Eventually it all became clear. After something of a frenzy in the flower bed by the hole, Oscar caught a mouse. As far as we knew it was the first one he had caught since he'd returned. He carried it into the lounge in his mouth, whereupon he dropped it. Mike, seeing what was going on, started to chase Oscar and the mouse round the lounge in a scene reminiscent of an episode of *Tom and Jerry*. Oscar was thoroughly enjoying playing with his quarry. Eventually, Mike managed to separate the two of them and take the poor little field mouse across the road, hopefully to go and join other members of its family. Oscar, meanwhile, was rather miffed that the mouse had been confiscated. He had been trying to catch it for months.

During the winter he was less inclined to want to go outside, preferring instead to spend his time on our bed or in the lounge. We bought a laser pointer and he had hours of fun chasing the red light around the room. He would pounce on it, then we'd turn the light off, but he was sure he had caught

190

it, so he sat there not moving his paws. Carefully he would edge them away so he could look at his catch, only to be surprised to find it was not there. As soon as he heard the click of the pointer he knew it was time for fun. We played this game night after night until eventually the battery ran out. This used up plenty of his energy. He was still only five years old and in any other circumstances would probably be doing a lot more exercise so it was important that he kept his movement up to keep his weight down.

After this exhausting game a sleep was inevitably the order of the day and there was no better place to flake out than in front of the log fire. We put a cushion on the hearth rug so he could lie on it and get the full benefit of the heat. He did like to get really close. Our concern was not so much him overheating, but that his feet might melt. We checked them constantly. The last thing we wanted was for Noel to think we were bad parents because his feet had got third-degree burns.

We were really looking forward to Christmas in 2011 as were all back together. Oscar was home and this would be the first one he had ever spent at the cottage (having spent the first one at New Era following his skin graft, then the following two in the UK).

We had to reposition the Christmas tree, which was no mean feat. For the previous few years we had positioned it in front of the French door in the lounge; however, this year we needed to be able to open the door to let Oscar out for his supervised visits to the garden. Our only option was to move the bookcase from the corner and put the tree there. This was much easier said than done, because not only is the bookshelf big, it also houses over 400 books and they weigh an absolute ton. It took us nearly three hours to unload the bookcase, move it four feet and then reload it. Needless to say, after Christmas we left it where it was.

On the night before Christmas Eve we held a party for our friends and neighbours and Oscar was the star of the show. Everyone knew his story but only a few had met him face to face. He totally lapped up the attention as people stroked him and examined his implants whilst Mike carried him round like a baby at a christening. It was a lovely evening and long after all the other guests had gone, our elderly next-door neighbours (who are also great party lovers) left. As we stood at the door saying goodbye to them, Oscar dashed past our legs, through the doorway and charged into the out-of-bounds area of the back courtyard.

After months of peeping through the cat flap he was finally out where he wanted to be. He was heading to the disused barn, which was exactly where we did not want him to go as it was full of old furniture, garden tools and brambles. Fortunately for us, but less good for Oscar, one of his prosthetic feet fell off. He continued to scamper about on three feet but we managed to scoop him up and take him back inside. We now had the problem of finding his foot in the darkness of the big, expansive courtyard. Our neighbour Jim turned on the floodlights to aid the search (our properties shared the courtyard) and we started looking for his tiny foot. We did have a spare pair, but we were not keen to use them unless absolutely necessary. We did eventually find it, thank goodness, and Mike quite rightly remarked that not many people could have said they went to bed so late that night because they were looking for their cat's foot.

We had a fabulous Christmas. My sister Victoria rang me to say that my niece had received the *Guinness World Records* book for Christmas and they were amazed to see Oscar was in it. He holds two records, one for being the first animal with two bionic leg implants and one for being the first animal to receive implants into moving joints.

All the cats had turkey for Christmas dinner, although this year we had finally made the decision not to buy them any presents. The garden centres were full to the brim with suggested gifts— squeaky mice with Santa hats, Christmas treats, turkey-and-ham flavoured chews, not to mention cat beds in the shape of Christmas puddings (tempting, but we resisted). The range for dogs was even greater and seemed to include a whole wardrobe full of seasonal outfits to dress the little pooches in. You had to wonder how there was any room for plants with the huge array of stock for pets.

As spring appeared and the days got longer and warmer, we could allow Oscar out for longer periods of time. If the weather forecast was fine Tracey would come up and sit with him so he could go out whilst we were at work. He liked sitting on the garden chairs, but only if the cushions were on them. As soon as we got a cushion from the cupboard he would trot along next to us, wait until it was in position on the chair then leap onto it and settle down for a snooze.

We were still in regular contact with Noel and updated him on Oscar's progress sending him photographs as requested so he could use them in his lectures. He also liked to see regular pictures of his feet and implants so he could check them and we also posted videos of him on YouTube from time to time. As Oscar's feet wore out, we sent Matt photos so he could examine exactly how and where they were worn. About every four months or so, Oscar received new feet and we would send the old ones back to Matt who remodelled them (after we'd got the new ones of course).

Living in Jersey we had to put a Customs declaration on the envelope stating the contents. I wonder what the officials made of seeing 'prosthetic cat's feet' written on our envelopes. We also had to state a value, which was nigh on impossible for such unique items. Most people who have seen Oscar's photographs on the Internet or in the paper will have seen his feet were white. After he had been home for several months, Matt sent us new feet in black, so finally he was fully colour coordinated.

Oscar continued to quite literally go from strength to strength. He was big and muscular. We kept a close eye on his weight (Noel's words were echoing in our ears whenever we gave him a treat—'I know you love him but don't let him get fat', he had told us in no uncertain terms) but nonetheless he had got very solid with muscle. He charged around the house at a rate of knots.

'Slow down, Oscar!' I shouted at him as he rushed past me in the hall. I was worried he was going to slip. You could hear him click clicking around the house as his back feet made contact with the stone floor in the hall and kitchen. He could never be a stealthy cat now.

One evening in the middle of summer, Oscar had been sitting outside enjoying the scented air when he suddenly charged in through the lounge. Mike had been keeping an eye on him, as although he sat out for long periods by himself, we never liked to get complacent and leave him for too long without supervision. I heard Oscar charge up the stairs, his speed seemed in no way impaired by the implants. Mike ran up after him and I didn't really think too much about it, as I was engrossed in the Olympics on the television. A few moments later Mike came down and went first into the garden and then to the kitchen before returning to the lounge to join me in watching the round-up of what had been another successful day for Team GB.

'Are you OK?' I asked casually, not really paying him too much attention.

'No. I've just been bitten by a mouse,' he replied. He explained that Oscar had caught it and taken it to our bedroom. When he had finally dropped it, Mike had picked it up by the tail but the mouse had managed to swing round and bite his finger.

'You're saying Oscar took a mouse to the bedroom?' I clarified as the magnitude of this statement hit me. My mouse phobia had in no way abated in the last few years of living in the country.

'Yes,' said Mike. 'It's so great that he's doing normal things.'

And it was. I was delighted that he was functioning like a normal cat, but the fact he was taking live mice upstairs did not exactly fill me with joy. A month or so later he caught a baby bird and took great delight in tossing it in the air before killing it, judging by the feathers everywhere. His newfound hunting prowess brought mixed feelings to us. I did not like the birds (or the mice for that matter) being killed as playthings, but I knew that

195

he was only acting instinctively.

As summer progressed we let Oscar stay out quite late at night. He had always been nocturnal and his plaintive cry at the door when he wanted to go out in the evening was hard to ignore. We let him out and turned on the outside light so we could see him more easily. He often sniffed about amongst the plants in the flower beds, making it very difficult to spot him.

One particular night in June, on the weekend of the Queen's Golden Jubilee, I was going to my friend Kim's wedding. I left Mike at home as I joined a group of girlfriends to enjoy the wonderful evening celebrations on this very special weekend. Everyone was in a buoyant mood at the wedding, not only because it was such a lovely, happy occasion, but also because it was the start of a four-day weekend and the Jubilee celebrations were creating a feel-good factor around the country. After a great evening, I returned home in the early hours of the morning and headed straight to bed, exhausted from dancing (and perhaps a bit too much wine).

'I'll be up in a minute. I'll just watch the end of this film and get Oscar,' shouted Mike to me as I took off layers of make-up and cleaned my teeth.

'Okey dokey. See you in a minute,' I replied as I got into bed. I was shattered and fell fast asleep, oblivious to the drama that was unfolding downstairs. Mike told me all about it the next morning.

'I went to get Oscar in and he wasn't there,' Mike said. 'I looked in the flower beds and there was no sign of him.' I sat up in bed and listened incredulously.

'I came back into the house in case he had come in and settled down somewhere but I couldn't find him,' he continued.

'Why didn't you wake me up?' I asked.

'Well, I thought it would be better to let you sleep. I didn't want you to panic.'

'Oh my God. What happened?' I asked trying to get to the nub of the story.

'As I couldn't find him in the house, I got the torch and went down the road, but there was no sign of him. I called and called but nothing.'

'It sounds like déjà vu,' I said casting my mind back to when we had found him in the culvert.

'In the end I got in the car and went for a drive around the lanes,' Mike continued. 'I came back, not having heard or seen anything and decided to go for another walk, this time going to other side of the field and there he was! I saw him in the exact spot where he had lost his feet.'

I couldn't believe that Oscar had managed to get out and get to the end of the field.

'He saw me and did a big walk round me as I tried to catch him, but he wouldn't let me,' said Mike. Goodness knows what anyone would have thought if they had driven past and seen a man in the field chasing something at three in the morning.

Mike explained that he gave up chasing Oscar and instead decided to head for home hoping that Oscar would follow. Oscar did exactly that, except when they got close to home, he ran and overtook Mike and let himself in through the cat flap as if he had never been away.

Unfortunately for Oscar, his escapade meant his outdoor life would have to be temporarily curtailed. Now he had escaped we would have to supervise him constantly so he would only be allowed out in short bursts. We also knew the only way he could have got out was to have climbed over the 6-foot-high fence. In many ways we were very proud, but it did give us a headache. First things first, though, we had to reinforce our defences.

The fence sits on a wall and we put panels of wood against the fence so he couldn't use the wall as a ledge to help propel him over to freedom and, of course, danger.

Oscar was unperturbed. The following week we were taking it in turns to mind him in the garden when suddenly he leapt right up and over the fence in front of our very eyes.

'Oh my God!' I screeched. 'He's gone again!' Mike grabbed the torch and was out through the door in a nanosecond calling Oscar's name. I followed close behind. We couldn't see him in the lane or the field. We called and called, but of course he did not come running. I mean, why would he? He had eaten dinner and was now ready for a night of adventure.

'He can't have gone too far,' I said, although we knew he could run at quite a pace when he wanted to. There didn't appear to be any obvious sign of him. It was possible he had gone into the field opposite, but the maize crop was still fairly short and at first glance he was not there. Perhaps he had trotted up to the main road or gone in the opposite direction down the lane? We had run out into the road probably no more than ten seconds after him, so we thought we would have seen him if he was heading off in either direction.

'The reinforcements did a fat lot of good,' huffed Mike. He had spent several hours the previous weekend cutting up the wood and screwing it on to the fence panels.

As Mike and I were deciding which route each of us should take to go and search for Oscar, I heard a rustling in Jim and Sheila's garden. I walked up their drive and sure enough, there was Oscar having a good old sniff in their fragrant borders.

'He's here!' I said to Mike in a whispered shout (if there can be such a thing).

I quickly realised that if I startled him, he would run off and potentially dash into the road. I crouched down and starting to talk to him in a gentle voice.

'Hello Oscar, what are you doing out here?' I said gently, extending my fingers in the hope he would come over for a head rub. He looked at me and obviously thought that Sheila's begonias were far more interesting and carried on sniffing and padding round the hedged garden as I edged closer and closer. I was not only worried about startling Oscar, the last thing I wanted was for Jim and Sheila to call the police because they thought there was an intruder in their garden. Oscar was ignoring me, but that was a good thing because it enabled me to get right up to him and sweep him up. I carried him back round to our house. He didn't struggle at all; I think he knew he was not meant to be out there.

The next day we revisited the fence situation. What we did not want to do was keep him inside all the time, so we decided to bolster the defences making it, we thought, insurmountable. Poppy did not help matters by periodically jumping onto the fence from the roadside, walking along it, tail in the air as if to say 'Look at me, na na na na na. You can't do this, I can!' Oscar would look up at her, totally bemused.

Finally, though, we were sure we had made the garden escape-proof. What we did not realise was that this was not going to be a problem at all in the not-too-distant future.

CHAPTER 19

SNAP. THE FINAL CHAPTER?

It was turning out to be the most amazing weekend. My sister Elizabeth, brother-in-law Daniel, and nieces and nephew Madeleine, Sophie and Will had come for a family weekend in Jersey. The weather had been glorious, hitting 28°C on the Friday. The previous day we'd been tourists and had taken the family to Jersey War Tunnels, a labyrinth of tunnels dug out by soldiers, civilians and prisoners during World War Two for the purposes of creating a command centre for the Germans and an underground hospital. It tells the story of Jersey during the Occupation. It was an eerie but fascinating attraction.

My sister Elizabeth and I were both very emotional at the end of the tour, having learned of the suffering of so many people on the island during this time. The men, on the other hand, were keen to press on and visit the many gun emplacements and bunkers that were dotted around the island. Mike, Daniel and Will thoroughly enjoyed our afternoon excursion, whilst Elizabeth and I admired the sea of heather that grew on the top of the cliffs. We failed to delight in what our menfolk clearly found so interesting.

We dropped the family members back at their hotel in the late afternoon so they could take a cooling dip in the outdoor pool, and Mike and I dashed home to prepare a few canapés to serve with champagne before we went out to dinner. It was the first time that Chris had met my nieces and nephews and despite being awkward teenagers, they all seemed to get on well.

On Sunday I got up early to prepare lunch for the eight of us and, as usual, Oscar was first up for breakfast. I put down a pouch of lamb chunks for him but he only had a few mouthfuls before running to the lounge to ask to be let out. I opened the door to a warm but foggy day. He scampered outside but ten minutes later he was back at his breakfast bowl. He followed his meal by having a scratch on the radiator cover before returning outside. I was not keen on his using the wooden radiator covers as a scratching post, not just because he was forever getting his claws caught in the decorative carved front, but more because I thought he was going to pull them over, such was his strength these days. That morning as I chopped and whipped and stirred, Oscar kept running between the kitchen and the garden. It was a wonder I didn't tread on him the number of times I stepped back to find him under my feet in the kitchen.

Time was getting on and my sister and family were due at noon, so I decided to go and rouse a weary Mike. As I approached the staircase Oscar was climbing up it. He was moving slowly and it didn't take me long to realise his foot had come off, so I picked him up and put him on the bed. Since Oscar had come home his feet had dropped off on a number of occasions and it wasn't something that worried us anymore. We just found the foot and screwed it on again and Oscar was very good at lying *in situ* until we found it. He was actually on his fourth or fifth set of feet since he had come back, not because they were lost, they had worn out just as our shoes do. This latest pair had very small holes where they attached to the implant (some had been bigger than others), thus ensuring they had a very tight fit to the titanium rod and so it was a surprise that one had fallen off. Nonetheless we did not think it was untoward.

'Can you stay with him while I go and look for his foot?' I said to Mike who proceeded to stroke him. We were used to having this sort of exchange of words. Oscar settled down and curled up with Mike.

'This will be fun,' I thought to myself. Being August the garden was very lush and looking for a black foot in the undergrowth was not going to be easy.

I walked into the lounge and there it was lying inside by the door.

I went to pick it up.

Shit. Disaster.

'Mike!' I yelled as I raced up the stairs. 'The implant's snapped off!'

Oscar's foot, which was meant to be the detachable part in case of emergency, had come off along with the bottom part of the implant. The titanium rod had sheared off at the point where it exited his stump. Oscar now had a pin inside his leg but no longer had the metal rod on which to attach the foot. He was also bleeding slightly.

I was panicking.

'This is a nightmare,' I said to Mike, while he continued to stroke Oscar, who seemed unperturbed by the drama.

'It's not good,' he agreed. 'Ring the vet and we'll take him down.'

I was shaking like a leaf as I scrolled through the phone numbers stored in the phone. Why couldn't I find New Era? I scrolled through again and found the number and, stumbling over my words, asked, 'Do you know Oscar, the bionic cat, the one with the implants?'

The lady paused and said, 'Yes, I know Oscar.'

'Great!' I replied and summarised what had happened. 'Can we bring him down?'

'Yes, of course. Where are you?'

'In Grouville.'

'How long will it take you to get here?' she asked.

'Five minutes.'

'Five minutes!' she exclaimed, seemingly surprised by my response.

'Yes.'

'We're closed at the moment so just ring this number when you're here and we'll let you in,' she advised.

Mike and Chris took Oscar down to the practice for his umpteenth visit and left him there to have his foot bandaged. Whilst he was there, the duty vet rang Peter. I asked Mike what Peter had said.

'He said "bugger",' replied Mike. Our thoughts exactly.

I tried my best to get a passable lunch together and rang Elizabeth to give her the update. The last thing I wanted to do was put a dampener on what had been an amazing weekend, but my emotions were barely in control. I just wanted to cry.

When Mike got back he rang Fitzpatrick Referrals in England.

'I spoke to Kate earlier. She said you were coming in,' said the woman on the end of the phone.

'Aha. I think I know what happened,' replied Mike, as he went on to explain.

Mike hadn't mentioned it to me, but when he and Chris arrived at New Era they seemed surprised to see him. I'd rung the wrong practice. In my panic and state of shock I had rung Fitzpatrick Referrals in England, no wonder they sounded surprised when I said we would be there in five minutes.

Mike was told by one of the clinicians that Noel wasn't working that weekend but she took all the details to pass on to him. An hour or so later they rang back asking for us to get the vet who was treating Oscar to contact him.

We had just finished lunch when the phone rang. Mike answered it and I could tell by his face it wasn't a good conversation.

'That was Emily, the duty vet, at New Era. Basically Noel could do another operation, cut the leg higher and put another implant in. It would cost £10,500. The other "option" is to have Oscar put down.'

It was too much to take in. Furthermore, Mike explained, apparently the company that made his particular implant no longer existed.

We didn't care about the money. Without verbalising it we both knew there was no way we could put Oscar through such an operation again. So, we knew where that left us.

At three o'clock we said goodbye to Elizabeth and her family and they headed to the airport while we went to fetch Oscar from New Era. Coincidentally, the nurse on duty, Leah, was the same one who had been responsible for his bandages before.

She had done a fine job but he did seem rather too trussed up.

We took him home, collecting Tracey on the way (she was coming round for tea) and let him out of the cat carrier. He couldn't walk. We put him in the middle of the carpet and he tried to stand up. He couldn't because his leg had been bandaged right to the top so there was no bend in it. He fell on his side. He tried again. The same thing happened. Then he made a noise I don't think either of us had ever heard before. He growled. Gentle little Oscar was not happy.

It must have been strange for him. Usually when his foot came off, we'd just screw it back on again. To him, that's what had happened today, but this time he'd been sedated and bandaged and he could not walk. It must have been hard for him to comprehend, if he even tried to.

Oscar couldn't settle. He tried to shuffle round the floor but he was frustrated that his bandaged leg would not cooperate. Every time he tried to get up he collapsed.

'It's no good,' said Mike, 'we need to take him back in.'

After ringing New Era and printing off some photos of how he was bandaged up previously, we once again went down to the vet's to hand him over.

Mike, Tracey and I reminisced about the last time we were in this situation three years ago.

'It's so difficult because he's not ill,' said Tracey. That was one of the worst parts of it. He was strong and fit and above all, very active. It seemed a damn cruel twist of fate.

'Look,' Tracey continued, 'we would have said goodbye to him three years ago had Oscar been taken to any other vet's surgery, or indeed if he had seen another vet instead of Peter. He could have died in the field from bleeding.'

We all agreed that Oscar had had a lot of borrowed time. Maybe it was time to let him go.

'It will be much worse for us,' I said. 'He won't know anything about it. Imagine if you weren't allowed to euthanise animals, he'd have a terrible life.'

'Well he's caught three mice and a bird in the last few weeks,' said Mike. 'He's had a fantastic summer.'

This was total déjà vu. We had had pretty much the same conversation in 2009.

After talking ourselves round in circles we all agreed that enough was enough for Oscar and that we would not agree to another implant.

We dropped Tracey home and went back to wait for Emily to call.

I answered the phone to her at about eight in the evening.

'I've taken off his bandages,' she reported. 'He's quite bruised, so if you don't mind, I'd like to keep him in tonight, so we can give him some pain relief and keep an eye on him.'

'No, that's fine,' I replied.

'Peter's on annual leave and has family over but

he's going to pop in tomorrow to see Oscar and to speak to Noel. Do you want me to call you in the morning?' she asked.

'No, there's no need until there's further news,' I replied. She checked with me about his current medication (which was none) and reassured me they would check him throughout the night.

'Actually, I will call you in the morning,' she advised me. We knew she would. The staff at New Era were excellent at keeping us up to date whenever any of the cats (usually Oscar of course) were inpatients.

Mike and I opened a bottle of wine for commiseration. Whichever way you looked at it, this was a very bad day for Oscar.

On Monday morning Emily called to say Oscar had had a comfortable night and was all right. She said she was going to try to speak to Peter and would let us know what he said.

Mike and I went to work, but I must admit my concentration levels were low. I kept reliving the moment I'd found his foot and broken-off implant on the lounge floor and how, once again, Oscar's life hung in the balance even though he was in excellent health.

On the way home from work we went to see Oscar. Louisa, one of the nurses, brought him through and explained that he was on opiates in case he was in any pain. They didn't want to give him the usual painkillers in case it had an adverse effect on his kidneys.

He was subdued but purring quietly. It was distressing to see him unable to walk. He seemed to have lost the confidence to stand on his three good (or goodish) legs and he was now extending his 'bad' leg out to the rear which was exactly how he'd held it when the initial amputation took place. This time, though, he didn't even seem to be trying to walk. He lay on his side on the examination table and moved by shuffling like a seal. Nonetheless he was looking round the room with curiosity and enjoyed a head rub and ear tickle.

We needed to speak to Noel and Peter.

Peter called us later that night. He said there was nothing more he could do for Oscar and the only people who could save him were a man in America or Noel. He, however, seemed as reluctant as we were to think about letting Oscar go.

'I think it's worth exploring further with Noel. I could try and repair the one that's broken but it wouldn't last. We could think about a prosthetic foot but because of the weight bearing issues it's very likely to fail. We'll have to see if we can come up with something. This is Oscar we're talking about,' said Peter.

'How old is he now?' he asked

'Five,' we replied in unison.

'He's still a baby,' Peter said. 'Look, I'm off till Thursday; I'll pop in to see him but in the meantime if you speak to Noel we can get a clearer picture of what's going on.'

We thanked Peter for calling us from his holiday and knew we could do nothing further until we'd spoken to Noel.

This finally happened the following evening when Noel called us at 11 p.m. (he had just finished a four-and-a-half-hour operation on a dog).

'I could do another operation,' explained Noel, 'but I'd have to amputate higher up the leg and put in a bigger implant. I think he deserves another chance.'

I had a pad full of questions.

'What sort of mobility will he have?' I asked.

'Limited,' said Noel bluntly.

'How long will the rehab be?' I asked reading from my list.

'Well it will take about four weeks to get the parts ready, then about three months of rehab.'

'Will you be happy for him to come back to Jersey?'

'Yes, for sure,' answered Noel.

'What's the prognosis for the current implant?'

'I don't know. He's the only cat with a bilateral so I can't say.'

Noel went on to reiterate the risks. The main one was the reason why this implant had failed. The *E. coli* and *Enterococcus* had caused the bone to die back, which meant the implant wasn't 'in' as much as it should have been. These two bacteria might still be present and there were no tests that could be run to ascertain if they were there. It was something that would only be discovered when they started the operation. Additionally, the implant might not take and there was also the risk from the anaesthesia; he had suffered problems with his kidneys previously. The choices we had were limited.

'Gosh, if we don't do it, it's almost like we're murdering him,' I commented.

'Look guys,' said Noel, 'you're caught between a rock and a hard place. You're going to be damned if you do and damned if you don't. Sleep on it and let me know your thoughts.'

We came off the phone even more confused. Speaking to Noel had given us a lifeline we didn't think was there. At the same time, we questioned if we should put Oscar through yet another operation which might not even work.

'What we have to remember is Oscar has already had three extra years and if he wasn't where he was and you weren't off work, then he would have died in that field.' I was trying to put things into perspective but it wasn't easy.

'I know, but he was great when we popped in earlier. He was bright-eyed and purry. He was very mellow,' said Mike.

'That's because he's full of drugs,' I replied.

'Look,' I continued, 'if we have him put down, at least he won't know anything about it. He won't go through any more pain.'

'At the same time if Noel thinks he can do something and he does seem keen to, surely we shouldn't deny Oscar the chance of carrying on with his life,' countered Mike.

'Yes, but he'll have restricted mobility. He's already got a limited life and it will be even more so,' I said. 'He can't roam freely in the fields or go over the fence which is what he wants to do,' I added. 'What if his other implant goes? Do we keep having his legs cut off higher and higher to accommodate new implants?'

We were talking but we weren't getting any closer to a decision.

'Let's talk to Peter on Thursday and go from there,' suggested Mike. The emotionally-charged conversation left us both in tears. I guess we never thought we'd be in this position again and it was so very difficult.

*　　　*　　　*

210

The next morning we were still unclear as to what we were going to do.

'What's your gut instinct?' Mike asked me, as we drove to work. There was barely any traffic as the schools were still on holiday and it was too early in the day for the tourists.

'I don't know. It will be so hard to actually do it. What are your thoughts?' I replied.

'The thing is,' he said, 'there's nothing wrong with him. You were right the other night when you said it would be murder to let him go.'

I did regret using the word 'murder'. It wouldn't be murder. It would be a humane way to end a life that would be severely limited. I was still thinking this might be the kindest route. The thought of all the upheaval of taking him to England and for him to go through all the trauma of surgery was almost too much to bear. It brought us back to something Noel had said several years ago. He never did things because they could be done; he did them because they should be done. But should we really do it to Oscar? He had no say in the decision. It would undoubtedly be a long and traumatic experience for him.

Later that morning Mike rang me to say Peter had taken a good look at Oscar and was erring towards the side of putting him through the operation. He explained that Noel had three years more experience, coupled with the fact that the implant would be larger as it was higher up the leg, so in effect, should be stronger. Despite this optimism, he said he wanted to do some blood tests before we moved forward with any decisions. If his kidneys were not functioning properly then

211

an operation could be potentially life-threatening. So we waited. In the meantime, news of Oscar's fate was spreading among friends, family and colleagues. Most of them seemed to agree it was not a decision they would like to make.

Oscar's results came back later that day. They were normal. It seemed that things were conspiring to take us in a certain direction.

After work we went to visit him again. He was so much brighter. He was still not standing up, although his bandages had been removed, but he seemed content to lie on the examination table and he purred non-stop for us.

Kerry, the head nurse and arguably Oscar's greatest fan, came through. She was convinced we should go through with the operation.

'There's something special about Oscar. Everyone who knows him agrees, but it's hard to explain to people who don't know him.' This was so true. Clearly we were hugely biased but he was such a spirited cat that he did seem to have more to live for.

Mike said to her, 'Peter said Oscar could live another ten years if it all went well.'

'Yes, but he could have a recurrence of the bacterial infection that happened last time,' I countered in my usual bad-cop way.

We spent about ten minutes chatting to Kerry before going home via the supermarket. Chris had passed his exams so we were having a celebratory meal of his choice. Being a teenage boy, this entailed pizza and ice cream.

That evening after dinner, Mike and I once more ran through the pros and cons of what to do for Oscar. We also received an email from Noel asking if we had made our decision and I emailed back to him, telling him we thought we would go ahead with the operation.

The next day we started looking into the logistics in more detail. Noel was available the following week if we definitely decided to go ahead, and luckily Mike still had plenty of annual leave left whereas I had virtually none. We thought it best if he took Oscar to England on his own.

We went to visit Oscar after work and he was even better that day and had a brief walk round as we stroked him. We had a quick word with Peter who said Noel had forwarded him the emails from us.

'So you think we should do it then?' I asked as Peter dashed through on his way to an operation.

'Well it is Oscar we're talking about,' he replied. That said it all.

We would have to see what Noel would say the next day. We still weren't clear on the costs and we wanted to be sure what we would be letting ourselves and Oscar in for.

We had moved a long way in five days from initially agreeing that we would not let Oscar have another implant. Now it seemed wrong not to let him have yet another chance. We decided to find out more about having the operation.

Noel duly sent us details of the costs. The operation would come to an estimated £12,000 but we would only have to pay a quarter of that. Only. This is where we had our first dilemma. We loved Oscar with all our heart but that was a lot of money. On the other hand, this was Oscar. We thought that so many people had done so much to help him along the way that we should find some way of getting the money. It would have been possible. Despite us having several personal loans for the house and car, not to mention the mortgage, two of the loans were coming to an end and I was sure we could have borrowed more money if necessary.

So, we decided that was what we would do. We would get the money together. We would take Oscar over the following week so Noel could get him measured up for a new implant and potentially new exoprostheses, or feet as we called them. Mike would use some of his annual leave. It was all falling into place. How lucky we were that so many people wanted to help Oscar get better; it was like he was immortal.

Whilst we were planning the practicalities we went to visit Oscar at New Era after work each day. The routine was the same; one of the nurses brought him through to a consulting room and placed him on the table where he sat in his usual unruffled manner. We stroked him and he purred; we proffered meaty stick treats but he didn't seem that interested. He seemed happy enough but really it was no life for him being locked up in a cage all day, especially when he wasn't actually ill.

The problem was that he couldn't be allowed to run around, as he would put too much weight on his left leg, his 'good' bad leg. His 'bad' bad leg was too short to touch the floor, so his weight was going through the one implant which was not a good thing. Poor old Oscar. We were very aware that final decisions needed to be made quickly. It was not fair on Oscar to keep him hanging around.

Each time we went to see him it also made us think whether we wanted him to spend at least a further three months in rehabilitation. This is how long Noel had estimated it would be. We were also concerned about the extra costs. The price, although firm for the operation, did not factor in any further surgery which might be required, or further rehabilitation, should it be needed. We knew Fitzpatrick Referrals were willing to give us a reduced rate, but potentially the costs could be huge and, of course, there was the risk that the operation might not work.

What concerned us most though was nothing to do with money. It was Oscar. Was it fair to put him through even more major surgery, which would involve a further amputation, a new implant, all the discomfort (not necessarily pain, although that too was a consideration) and then the long road to recovery? We ummed and we ahhed. What we really wanted to know was what he wanted. On the one hand he was in the prime of life, fit and vital. On the other he had a life-limiting condition which, even if surgery was successful, would lead to an even more restricted life than he had now. Noel had told us his mobility would definitely be restricted, he did not know to what degree, but nonetheless he was a cat, not a person. He needed to be mobile and he needed to jump. I couldn't see how he could have a life totally at ground level. Like all cats he likes to jump on chairs and beds and sofas. He likes walking on tables. Especially when it is a) laid for a dinner party or b) covered in paperwork. Both of these options worked better if he had just come in from the rain and had muddy little paws.

We really did not know what to do for the best. Were we being cruel to put him through another operation or were we being cruel not to, when we already knew he had great determination and a real will to live? We just could not decide. We thought about other options. People asked why he couldn't just potter about on three legs; after all, cats can live very successfully with a limb missing. We explained to them that it would put too much pressure on the other leg, which could ultimately result in his implant failing on that side.

We thought about getting a different sort of prosthetic. Again the same problem arose, as he would not be able to have an even distribution of weight. We looked into getting a little trolley with wheels on it. Funnily enough, when we googled 'trolleys for disabled cats', the first thing that came up was a website called www.oscardog.it. I also read about a cat called Hector who was paralysed in his hindquarters but lived happily for several years with such a trolley before succumbing to an unrelated cancer. Seemingly, his placid nature meant he adapted well to having such a mobility cart. Oscar had that sort of nature. He took everything that came his way with patience and tolerance.

Realistically, though, we did not think that would be fair on Oscar. The whole reason we went through with the surgery in the first place was to afford him as good a quality of life as possible. Having a mobility cart or trolley would not enhance his life. It would just mean he was alive.

By now Oscar had been at New Era for two weeks and all the time we were still deciding what to do. Eventually they told us we could bring him home as long as we restricted his movement. We borrowed a cage from our friends and set it up with a litter tray, bed, food and water as well as a brand new hoggy and Oscar's little red mouse. He seemed to be delighted to be home, but when he started meowing to be let out we felt very mean leaving him in the cage. The girls at New Era had warned us this would happen. They said that he was used to being in the cage with them, but at home he was used to being up and about. Being Oscar, though, he must have known it was for his own good and he settled down on his new towel and blanket bed.

We let him out each day for a stretch and day by day he seemed to be more mobile. He was hopping about on three legs as if was the most natural thing in the world. On the one hand we were really pleased as he could go outside and sit in front of his favourite hole by the fence or he could just lie on the cushion from the lounger, which we put on the floor. On the other hand we recognised that every step he took was potentially weakening his remaining implant.

His mobility was definitely restricted too. One of his favourite places to sit is on the leather dining chairs. In fact, it has been a constant source of inspiration to me that he often sits in a chair next to me as I write this book. One evening he went to leap onto the chair is the usual manner, obviously not realising he had no propulsion. The net result was his front claws were in the leather of the seat and the rest of his body was dangling over the edge. He was effectively stuck. I managed to 'unhook' him but it brought it home to us that he could never roam freely about the house. It was just too risky.

As the days passed we knew we had to decide what to do. We spoke to friends and family and they understood our dilemma. Mike and I talked ourselves round in circles about it.

We finally decided that the kindest thing for Oscar would be to have him put down. Not murdered. Just gently put to sleep. He had been through enough. We told Noel and it was clear he wanted to operate although he understood our decision. We told Peter, who was also sad at the decision, but at the same time understood the reasoning behind it.

All we had to do now was arrange a date. We thought about the end of that week, as we didn't want to do it on a weekday when we had work the next day. We knew we would be really upset. We spoke to Peter again. He was going to America for two weeks so we wanted to wait for him to come back as he had said to us that whilst he did not want to put Oscar to sleep, he did not want anyone else to do it either. On the day before he left he rang Mike.

'Can you give Oscar to me for one day? I just want to see if I could possibly make a prosthetic for him. I'm not sure that I can, but I'd love to try.'

Mike immediately agreed.

In the meantime we decided we would let Oscar have as free a life as would be safe for him. Tracey came up each day whilst we were at work and let him out in the garden. In the evening we let him roam around the house. At night he slept on our bed, so he could have a good old stretch. We still had his cage which we put him into if we thought he had been running around too much, and if we went out we always put him in it. He had two litter trays, one in his cage for emergencies and a larger one in the kitchen which he favoured. His aim was rubbish and the litter tray in his cage was too small for him really, but space was limited. Lou thought it was great news she could use his litter tray too. Before the accident his tray was enclosed and he'd climb into it through a flap similar to a cat flap, but we decided it would be too hard for him to get in and out of, so we were back with an open one. Lou found this far easier to use than having to go outside. She's not known as Lazy Lou for nothing.

In the evening, Oscar often climbed into the cage of his own accord to curl up on his bed. Lou also sneaked in to nibble on his bowl of biscuits (although never when Oscar was there). We knew that if he broke his other implant then it really would be game over, but for now we would see how he got on with his latest restrictions.

We always carried him up and down the stairs to assist him. One Saturday evening when he had been home for about a fortnight, we thought he was lying in the hall as he loved looking out through the cat flaps. He wasn't there. We checked the kitchen. He wasn't there either. Mike went upstairs and we have no idea how he managed it, but somehow Oscar had managed to jump onto our bed and had curled up to go to sleep. He obviously fancied an early night.

*   *   *

So how does this story end? When I wrote the first draft of this book, there was a happy ending. Oscar was living as full a life as could be hoped. His implants and prosthetic feet were working better than we could ever have imagined. He was healthy, happy and active. When our friends popped round they seemed surprised at just how nimble he was. It was literally a matter of weeks before my final deadline that everything changed. But this is real life and real life does not always end how we hope.

219

I honestly do not know what Oscar's fate will be. But I know that when people say that Oscar must be the luckiest cat in the world, we think the truth of the matter is that we have been the luckiest owners. Not only has Oscar been afforded the greatest veterinary care available both in Jersey and the UK, and arguably in the world, but he has also been the most endearing, charming, friendly little cat that we have ever known. We love all our cats, but we will never have one as special as Oscar ever again.

BIBLIOGRAPHY

Printed resources

A Day in the Life of Oscar the Cat, David M. Dosa, M.D., M.P.H., *N. Engl. J. Med*. 2007; 357:328–329 July 26, 2007

Online resources

The Indoor-Outdoor Debate Revisited. Should Cats be Allowed Outdoor Without Supervision? by Franny Syufy, About.com Guide

How To Train Your Cat to Walk With a Leash By Franny Syufy, About.com Guide

http://www.bbc.co.uk/news/10404251

http://www.csicop.org/superstition/library/black_cats/

http://www.newscientist.com/article/dn17455-hungry-cats-trick-owners-with-baby-cry-mimicry.html

http://www.pet-insurance.co.uk/blog/news/RSPCA-encourages-people-to-adopt-a-black-cat-801429281/

http://www.smosh.com/smosh-pit/articles/robo-cats-are-set-take-over-world

http://www.telegraph.co.uk/family/pets/8157908/
The-Bionic-Vet-he-can-rebuild-them.html

http://www.thecatsite.com/a/the-mystique-behind-black-cats

http://www.thesun.co.uk/sol/homepage/news/3792120/The-paw-relations.html

http://www.wayofcats.com/blog/theres-nothing-wrong-with-bionic-cats/8440